THE LOO FALCONRY

Dedicated to the incredible peregrine

THE LOO FALCONRY

The Royal Loo Hawking Club 1839-1855

BY DR. J. W. M. VAN DE WALL

hancock house

ISBN 0-88839-576-0

Cataloging in Publication Data

Wall, J. W. M. van de (Joost Willem Marinus), 1917-
The Loo falconry : the Royal Loo Hawking Club, 1839-1855 / by J.W.M. van de Wall.

Translation of: De Valkerij op het Loo.
Includes bibliographical references and index.
ISBN 0-88839-576-0

1. Royal Loo Hawking Club--History. 2. Falconry--Netherlands--Apeldoorn--History--19th century. I. Title.

SK321.W3413 2004 799.2'32'06049218 C2004-904166-5

Printed in Korea—PACOM

Color plates: Courtesy of *The House of Orange-Nassau Historic Trust,* The Hague
Translation credit: Translated from Dutch to English by Mrs. A. Lents-Michaelis.

Published simultaneously in Canada and the United States by

HANCOCK HOUSE PUBLISHERS LTD.
19313 Zero Avenue, Surrey, B. C. V3S 9R9
(604) 538-1114 Fax (604) 538-2262

HANCOCK HOUSE PUBLISHERS
1431 Harrison Avenue, Blaine, WA 98230-5005
(604) 538-1114 Fax (604) 538-2262
Web Site: www. hancockhouse. com
email: sales@hancockhouse. com

Contents

Acknowledgements

I feel highly indebted to Her Majesty Queen Beatrix who gracefully allowed me access to the Royal House Archive to study documents and objects in relation to the subject of this book.

Mr. A. G. Ubels, chief keeper of the records, assisted me in a most obliging way. I gratefully express my thanks to all those who assisted me by word and deed and provided me with many facts and items: Mr. E. Van de Beek; the Hon. H. C. Beelaerts van Blokland Mr. P. C. J. M. Bekkers; Mrs. I. Blankenbijl-Schaafsma; Dr. and Mrs. Bonte; Mrs. Bots-Gooden; Mr. H. A. Daendels; Mrs. J. Enklaar, assistent Prof. Utrecht University; Dra. A. M. L. E. Erkelens, State Museum Palace Het Loo; Mr. J. Van Gerven; Mr. F. Hoppenbrouwer; Mr. F. A. Kleyn; Mr. A. P. W. M. Kosten, former librarian of the State Museum of Natural History, Leiden University; Dr. J. M. P. van Oorschot, historian of the municipality of Nijmegen; Major F. C. H. Rhebergen; The Hon. J. W. C. Sloet van Oldruitenborgh; Mr. A. F. Stroink and many others who motivated and supported me.

I am particularly indebted to Lady L. R. M. van Everdingen-Meyer; Mr. E. Reinders, former-chief steward of her Majesty's Royal Shoot at The Loo; Mr. P. Tuijn, historian, director of the Museum of Game and Game-Management, who kindly studied and surveyed the manuscript and provided me with many valuable annotations.

And, finally, I am greatly indebted to the staff of the State Museum Palace Het Loo who gave me the opportunity to publish this book in connection with the exhibition of the same title. The editorial activities and support of the curator of the museum, Dr. E. Elzenga, have greatly assisted me.

THE AUTHOR
SECOND EDITION 2003

After many years, a dear wish at long last became fullfilled. Many interesting new facts and items came into light. Dr. Nick Fox was interested and helped me establish friendly contact with publisher David Hancock.

I am very much in debt to Mrs. A Lenz-Michaelis who translated "de Valkerij op 't Loo," in the most perfect style. I am very greatful to Mrs. May Hogenboom who assisted me in preparing the edition. Last, but not least, my daughter-in-law Dominique van de Wall-Lehmann was of invaluable help in preparing the final edition.

LEUSDEN 2004
THE AUTHOR

Preface

Falconry at The Loo was practised in a spectacular and colourful way and society life at the palace was no less sparkling and vivid. After the activities of the Royal Loo Hawking Club ceased, the last sparks soon died, and so the Club passed into oblivion. True enough, many historical data were saved, but all too often they were hidden in unknown or barely accessible archives. It is remarkable that such a magnificent, illustrious and international society was never known as widely and profoundly as might be expected. In falconry circles its existence is still vaguely known. The Club was mentioned in some books and papers, but detailed knowledge was confined to but a very few investigators. In 1843 Prof. Hermann Schlegel and A. H. Verster van Wulverhorst began to compile their famous work *Traité de Fauconnerie* and completed it in 1853. They wrote in French and about one hundred copies were printed. Lt. Col. N. J. A. P. H. van Es[1] however, stated that the elephant-folio edition numbered to less than a hundred copies, of which no more than fifty are complete. The price of this edition was 210 Dfl, a considerable sum, bearing in mind that the buyer had to find his own bookbinder, and that the salary of an assistant falconer in those days came to 280 Dfl. per annum. Some of the copies disappeared into libraries, others were damaged beyond repair when the French texts were discarded and the extremely fine illustrations by Wolf used for other purposes. As a source of information the original *Traité de Fauconnerie* is accessible to only a few. Moreover, it provides little information concerning the Royal Loo Hawking Club, while falconers, falcons and their training are discussed at length.

In 1908 Van Es published an elaborate historiography in twelve folio-volumes about his army units, the renowned Mounted Artillery Corps. One of these volumes was dedicated to equestrian sports in general and another to hawking parties at The Loo and the equestrian activities of the Club's members. Van Es, contrary to Schlegel and Verster van Wulverhorst, provides us with elaborate information about the members of the Club and their activities. However, this book is even rarer than the *Traité de Fauconnerie*. It was written in Dutch and we must assume that the edition amounted to only fifteen copies. This book became extremely rare because some copies were damaged or lost.

In 1937 *Falconry in the Netherlands* by Prof. A. E. H. Swaen[2] was published. In this general survey the author dedicates a chapter to the Royal Company at The Loo, using the scanty information that could be drawn from the *Traité de Fauconnerie*. Apparently history was loath to yield its secrets, for shortly after publication an all-consuming fire destroyed press and storage, and so this book also became rare.

At long last, in 1974, the historian Dr. J. M. P. van Oorschot[3] threw new light on the subject in his excellent thesis about Dutch falconry since the seventeenth century. No more detailed and elaborate study on the history of falconry has appeared to date.

The impression we can glean from the studies mentioned above would be incomplete without the sublime collection of watercolours and sketches by J. Wolf, J. B. Sonderland, P. L. Dubourcq and others who recorded pictorially all the facts and events of falconry at The Loo. Prince Alexander commissioned Sonderland and Dubourcq to sketch the scenes in watercolours and pencil drawings respectively. Today they form part of the historical collections of the House of Orange-Nassau.

I Introduction to Falconry

The falcon mounts to heaven with the speed of a prayer
and stoops with the speed of destiny.
—An old Arab saying

Falconry is the art of using wild falcons to capture wild birds and animals. Contrary to "'subsistence-hunting," man's economy of surviving, falconry is an "expressive emotional human activity." When mankind became impressed by the aristocratic stature of the falcon and the beauty of its flight, falconry came into being. Certain cultural development is essential and indispensable for its development. Falconry flourished only among peoples of high cultural standing. There is no indication that primitive hunters used hawks to hunt or, let alone, enjoy the beauty of their flight.

If it is true that India's plains were populated from a central Asiatic cradle, we may assume that falcons were carried over the Kyber-Pass on the glove just alike their aristocratic masters in their palanquins. About India and Persia we are better informed. Numerous Persian miniatures show us falconers dressed in costly garments their birds exquisitely portrayed, with jesses[4] and halsbands[5] of fine silk. From here falconry found its way to the Arabian World. Later, when a certain degree of cultural development originated in western Europe, falconry also settled there. Falconry and hunting belonged to the first privileges that the social order of those days imposed upon its rulers. The strong social divisions were consequently extended to the hawks. Only kings were allowed to carry the very costly gyrfalcons[6], lesser nobility and clergy had to content themselves with the lower ranking shortwings[7]. Regulations were elaborate and extended to the minute details.

During the Renaissance falconry, both literally and figuratively, soared high in western Europe. Falcons escorted the nobles and their ladies when going to church and on military campaigns. There was no question of popularisation in those days; royalty and nobility kept all rights to themselves till the end of the eighteenth century. The French Revolution, however, put an end to this. Day by day war, revolution and the subsequent lack of funds increased their detrimental effect on the "King of Sports."[8] The development of sophisticated shooting guns may have contributed to its downfall. Finally, the encroaching cultivation of waste lands made it physically impossible to continue falconry in the same traditional way.

For the sake of clarity, falconry and Haut Vol[9] were almost identical in those times. The designation Haut Vol meaning high flight originated when

The old Loo palace during the time of the Royal Loo Hawking Club. The club members would gather in the north tower. Watercolour by Jan G. Smits (1823-1910).
Royal Collection. Koninklijk Huisarchief The Hague.

the French language was commonly used in the courts of royalty and nobility. The name was not known in earlier times. It is unlikely that the Haut Vol in mediaeval times, compared to the practice in the late renaisaance, was of more importance than an incidental flight at a bird "en passage."

The exceptional character of Haut Vol was based on two fundamental facts namely:

1 The difference in wingloading of the two combatants—heron and falcon. The heron (low wingloading) is a master in quick climbing and so tries to evade.

2 The falcon (high wingloading) has a slow rate of climbing and so is forced to overcome the law of gravity to obtain a stooping position for the attack. The heron in the meantime is climbing quickly from the moment the falcon starts from the falconer's fist.

The Haut Vol furthermore requires a very large heronry (The Loo had an estimated 1,000 pairs) and rich feeding grounds, both separated by vast plains where the aerial tournament finds an ample stage to perform.

The passage of the herons takes place in late spring and early summer when the hungry young birds were awaiting their parents to feed them. The "season" coincides with the moulting period of the falcons.

The falcons, contrary to the expectance of some of the gyrfalcons, were not the best performers. Peregrines defended their status as prima ballerinas very well.

The back of the The Loo Palace, ca. 1837.
By Andreas Schelfhout (1787-1870).
Royal Collection. Koninklijk Huisarchief The Hague.

It was Haut Vol that declined, not falconry in a less restricted sense. In the last century falconry passed from the hands of professionals into those of able amateurs. Moreover the sport could dispose of other facilities.

The last stronghold of those falconers who had mastered the art of catching and training was in Valkenswaard, situated amidst vast moors. The hurricane of the French Revolution had passed by without inflicting too much direct damage. On the first of October, name-day of their Patron St. Bamis, the falconers used to go to the huts for a period of two months to catch hawks. During this time they started "manning"[10] the freshly caught birds. In spring they returned to their royal employers with their more or less trained pupils to practise the Haut Vol. Thus, in a strict sense, falconry was not practised at Valkenswaard. When the Haut Vol on the continent fell into decline, there were still modest possibilities in England, and therefore falconers moved to the British Isles.

It was not as yet realised that in England, too, cultivation was rapidly diminishing the areas suitable for the Haut Vol. The definite end of the sport, the clearly defined discipline of falconry as we know it, was threatening also in England. Falconer Jan Bots from Valkenswaard, master of the art of flying the heron (en passage), suggested to investigate the possibilities the Royal Domain The Loo perhaps could offer. (We shall meet Jan Bots again.)

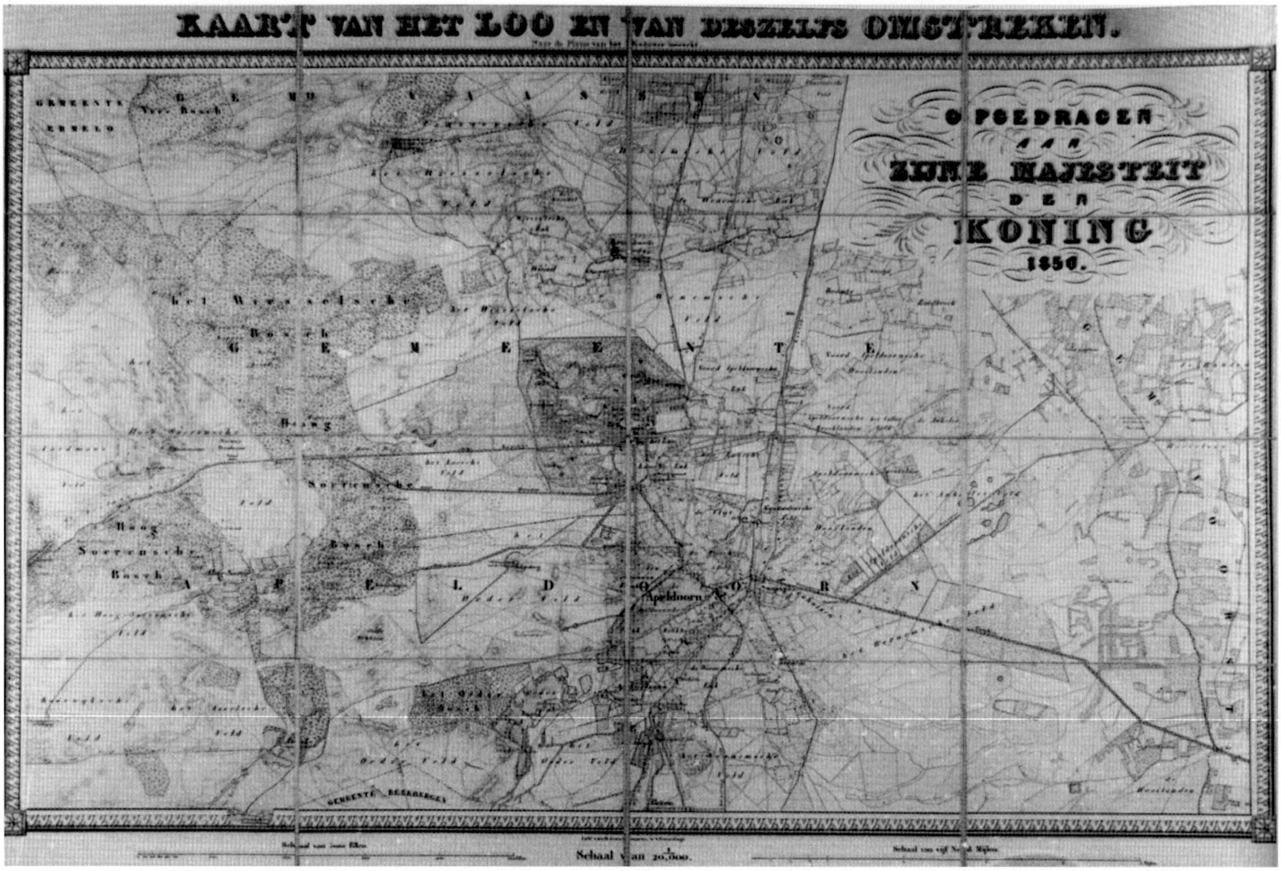

Map of the domain Het Loo, 1850. Litho by H. J. van Leeuwen.
Paleis Het Loo Nationaal Museum Apeldoorn.

II The Origin of the Club

—Dedicated to the late Gerrit van Nie

A clear distinction must be made between the international society assembled in the Royal Loo Hawking Club and the way the sport was practised at many western European courts until deep into the eighteenth century. In fact the society consisted of and was founded by passionate advocates who wished to practise falconry for its intrinsic merits. The most important motive was to continue the flight on heron and kite, rather than maintain and preserve falconry as such. The Haut Vol derived its attraction from the fact that herons, relatively slow flyers but good climbers, had to resort to mounting to such heights as to insure a literally lofty tournament. The hawks were handicapped by the fact that they were forced to mount from ground-level and to surmount the high-flying herons. These enforced tactics brought a very essential and conspicuous dimension to the Haut Vol.

In the eighteenth century kite and black kite[11] greatly diminished in numbers. Later the heron followed, victim of encroaching cultivation and the resulting drainage of wetlands. The number of fields suitable to the Haut Vol diminished, and this meant that its advocates had to travel farther and farther to attend the spectacle. Today it is rather difficult to imagine, but travelling in those unsettled days was hazardous, especially on the continent and when longer stays were necessary.

In the British Isles falconry was chiefly pursued with grouse hawks trained to wait on. A family of Flemish descent, the Flemings of Barochan Castle, was well known in this respect. Towards the end of the eighteenth century they founded The Renfrewshire Subscription Hawks, a society for falconers and those interested in falconry. The name speaks for itself—as a subscriber one could take part in the flights. On Fleming's death in 1812 Sir John Maxwell succeeded him and managed the Club until 1830, when it came to an end. The hawks used were eyasses, almost exclusively trained to wait on. At the same time there was another Society in England engaged in falconry. For these gentlemen, however, the issue was the Haut Vol. This sport was passing into oblivion on the continent and in the British Isles, too, it was rapidly diminishing. Around 1772, the exact date[12] is not yet definitely known, either Col. Thornton (1754–1823) or Lord Orford established a society under the significant name of The Confederate Hawks of Great Britain obviously based on the saying united we stand. It was clear that without cooperation the Haut Vol was doomed. Although there was a lack of falconers who mastered the art

Col. Thornton, ca. 1772, founder of the Confederate Hawks of Great Britain.
Valkerij en sigarenmakerij Museum Valkenswaard.

of the flight at the heron, this could easily be remedied. On the continent, and particularly in Valkenswaard, there were many falconers whose prospects were seriously threatened. So it happened that Frans van den Heuvel entered Thornton's service and was the first to introduce the Dutch school in England. Later, many more from Valkenswaard were to follow. Contacts with the English school were soon established and experiences exchanged. The English flew grouse with eyasses, the Dutch herons with passage hawks. The English adopted the Dutch type of jesses and the Dutch, in all probability, became acquainted with flying at hack.

For convenience sake the Society of the Confederate Hawks was soon called The Falconers' Club. It was a small body of advocates that, as kites became scarce, increasingly turned to flying herons. In 1781 Thornton resigned and was succeeded by Lord Orford who died in 1792. Wilson of Didlington, later Lord Berners, took his place and under his guidance the Club moved to High Ash near Didlington in Norfolk (High Ash Club). When Berners died in 1838 the Club was already falling into decline and finally ceased. For those enthousiasts who remained loyal to the sport, this was difficult to swallow. In particular Edward Clough Newcome, born in

1810 and the soul of the enterprise, would not concede that the flight at the heron should cease. This gentleman, who played a most important role in falconry, first made his acquaintance with the sport when, on Wilson's invitation, he attended the flights at Didlington. It was love at first sight; he threw himself heart and soul into falcons and falconry. In 1838 he had in service a five-year-old passage tiercel, called Will o' the Wisp, that flew rooks well—quite an achievement for a tiercel. About 1850 he attracted attention for his success in flying merlins on mounting larks. It was remarkable that he was not very interested in the art of waiting on, preferring to shoot partridge on his Norfolk estate rather than flying them with a tiercel over his pointer.

We shall meet Newcome again. Suffice it to say that after the closing down of the Royal Loo Hawking Club he continued to practise falconry with great zeal. In 1863 this led to the foundation of the Old Hawking Club under his animated leadership. Major Hawkins Fisher (1901) said of him: "A Norfolk squire, the best of gentleman-falconers now living."

John Godolphin Duke of Leeds was also a very passionate falconer and, like Newcome, destined to play an important role at The Loo. When he was still Marquess of Carmarthen he flew both eyasses and passage falcons on grouse, partridge and woodcock. It is known that in 1838 his tiercels The General and Macduff and the falcons Pearl and Diamond killed 316 pieces of game. This shows the great ability of both falconer and falcons. In 1845 he sent his falconer John Pells to Iceland to catch gyrfalcons. Pells was lucky and caught fifteen under his bownet. Eight of them were destined for The Loo but did not meet expectations. Leeds kept seven birds himself. They were trained to fly hare but again could not claim success. The best gyr he had was a jerkin called Morock or Marock although he would not fly with another bird. The tale goes that Morock was lost[13] when Leeds, as a guest of his friend Newcome, was flying in Norfolk. Shortly afterwards, falconers on The Loo recognised and caught him.

The lady, frightened by a heron accidentally strikes her husband in the face with her cane.
J. Sonderland Royal Collection.

During this period two other gentlemen were of importance: Stuart Wortley and d'Offémont. In a way they can be regarded as quartermasters of the society that was about to assemble at The Loo. The Hon. Stuart Wortley[14], youngest son of Baron Wharncliff, was the descendent of an old English family. He died in 1844 at the early age of forty-two having been able to attend the events of The Loo for only a few years. Auguste d'Offémont was a gentleman of old French lineage. He could claim a pedigree dating from the fourteenth century and lived in the castle of the same name, practising hawking with hawks from Valkenswaard. He also made his name as austringer and educated the next generation in this branch of the sport. Those days were far from uneventful in France and when practising falconry on a large scale, tranquillity was necessary. So he resorted to England and joined the Falconers' Club. He was not averse to publicity as is evident from a practical joke—he had his falcons flying pigeons on the Place des Tuilleries in Paris.

After the death of Lord Berners and the liquidation of the Falconers' Club in 1838 it was these gentlemen in particular who tried to find means to continue the Haut Vol, and it was the falconer Jan Bots who showed them the way. Bots knew the advantages The Loo could offer and advised them to investigate. Difficulties were unlikely to arise. King William I and his son, Crown Prince William, aide de camp to the Duke of Wellington, had been admitted to London society during their exile. They became intimate friends with the Duke of Leeds, as is evident from a letter from the Duchess of July 21, 1847, in which she addresses William II, former Crown Prince William, as "My dear King of Holland." In this letter she points out that it would be good for Prince Alexander's health to stay with them during the deer-shooting season. As a matter of fact in 1838, the year in which Bots first mentioned The Loo, Prince Alexander had already stayed with the ducal family.

Baron van Tuyll van Serooskerken, like his father, chamberlain to the King and well known in London society circles may have been of help. Thanks to personal recommendations the way to King William I was thus free of any obstacles. Soon afterwards the King received a request from Stuart Wortley and d'Offémont for permission to explore the possibilities the Royal Domain Het Loo could offer. Stuart Wortley was welcome but not so d'Offémont.

On July 4, A. H. Baron Sloet van Oldruitenborgh, adjutant to Prince Alexander and afterwards to his brother King William III, in his capacity of Chief-Steward of his Majesty's shoots in the Northern Provinces, addressed himself to Count van Rechteren. This gentleman was chamberlain to His Majesty King William I and entrusted with the official Direction of Hunting and Shooting at the Seignory The Loo:

> I see no objection to recommending the King to grant Mr. Stuart Wortley (14) the required permission. I suppose that he requires this permission only for himself because if the friend, who with said gentleman paid his respects to Your Honour, should wish to practice falconry in and around the forestry of Souren, his nomination could not be made without mentioning his name. The art of falconry involves the assistance of falconers and these come as servants. If falconers intend to practice privately they should be placed in the category of hunters and need licences too.
>
> I invite You to inform me about these two points. After receiving Your answer I shall authorise the Gentleman Forester of the 3rd district to register the request.

It is clear: d'Offémont, who together with Stuart Wortley called upon van Rechteren, was not as yet able to pass the barrier. Formally, too, the case was still incomplete. On August 27, Sloet let van Rechteren knew that: "He, the

Sutler, accompanying the party to the field.
J. Sonderland Royal Collection.

said gentleman, will have to be provided with falconers' licences as prescribed by law, in which no distinction is made between herons and game.

Sloet, meanwhile, willing to grant both gentlemen their licences on authority of van Rechteren, had informed the King of all this. Probably when van Rechteren informed His Majesty about the verbal request, the latter had not listened with much attention and answered with lack of interest that the gentlemen could go ahead. When, however, matters had reached the point of being put in black and white he suddenly took offense at d'Offémont: who is he? Sloet had to provide some information. He in turn asked van Rechteren to inform him, assuming that he would probably know more about it:

> The request of Messrs. Stuart Worthley (!) and d'Offémont, being brought to the attention of the King, His Royal Highness has expressed the wish to be informed about the relations of said gentlemen; the social standing of the last mentioned; what caused their wish to practice falconry during four months and why they chose the surroundings of The Loo for this purpose. I shall be very pleased to receive sufficient information from Your Lordship to present to the King.

While van Rechteren attempted to obtain more information about d' Offémont, Sloet had become somewhat wiser but still didn't know enough:

> September 26th 1838. In a private message from Valkenswaard there is no mention of falcons being trained here on behalf of a French Prince d'Offermont, I wonder if the name d'Offémont is incorrect and should perhaps be d'Offermont or d'Offrémont. Would Your Lordship be so kind as to inform me regarding this matter or otherwise investigate if necessary?

In the meantime van Rechteren had finished his research as shown by a letter from Sloet:

> October 8th 1838. I have the honour to return to You the visiting card of the Hon.

Auguste d'Offémont in compliance with the request expressed in Your letter of September 29th.

So, at last matters were settled. A simple visiting card opened the gates to The Loo, as easy and as difficult in those days as in ours. By virtue of rescript of October 19, the licence to practice falconry on heron in and around the Soeren forestry was issued to the gentlemen under condition that they should act strictly according to regulations of the game laws. Sloet, however, had not realised that in March herons were busy building their nests and so could not be flown at. He expected the gentlemen at the end of March or early in April but no message reached him. In a confidential letter he again addressed himself to Van Rechteren, asking him if he perhaps knew more and whether the request for the licences had already been forwaded to the Chief Forester of the Third District in the Province of Gelderland. If all documents had not reached the bureau of the Registrar of Deeds at Apeldoorn on time, he was willing to send provisional licences which could be issued after deposition of the amount due at the office of said officer. It took until June 26 before the Registrar of Deeds could report that the rights were paid for.

The gentlemen met with succes. Bots and his servants had a good catch in the autumn and appeared at The Loo with eighteen falcons, two of them tiercels. The exact number of birds is uncertain; another version indicates twenty-one birds: possibly Bots had also three birds on the cadge from the last season in England (High Ash)[15]. It is also possible that Newcome took three birds along. Anyhow, the score of 104 herons was impressive. Everything went so prosperously that the gentlemen lost no time in requesting prolongation of their licence in a letter of d'Offémont dated July 4, 1838:

> The permission His Majesty benevolently granted us for this year is on the point of expiring. We were pleased to witness 104 herons brought down. Mr. Wortley and I feel obliged to let Your Majesty know of our respectful gratitude for this favour. We reverentially request You to have a new licence issued to us for the Haut Vol in the coming year. If You kindly grant this request, we propose to take action immediately to obtain superior falcons from Norway.

This letter was also signed by Stuart Wortley. The King had no objection and his grandsons, Crown Prince William and his brother Prince Alexander, would wholeheartedly have supported the plans.

It was not, as might be expected, Stuart Wortley and d'Offémont who went to Norway to catch gyrfalcons but Edward Newcome and Vincent Baron van Tuyll van Serooskerken.[16] In the company of Bots and after a journey of five days, they arrived at Christiania (Oslo) and from there travelled the old route to Hjerkinn, Dovrefjell, today known as The Kings Highway. They were lucky and returned with three gyrfalcons[16a].

tribution was fixed at 100 Dfl. per annum or more. Hopes were cherished that many would pay more, but it was not to amount to much.

Subsequently the Seignory Het Loo was appointed as the location for future events. The President, Prince Alexander, was authorized to appoint a supporting secretary and treasurer. Furthermore sporting events were not allowed on Sundays. Article no. 10 testified both of practical insight and undesirable experiences: "To prevent delay in the proceedings, none but the falconers are allowed to ride horses belonging to the club." Matters like ballot and expulsion, for example, were courteously omitted in the draft. On April 10, the provisional draft regulations were signed in The Hague by Prince Alexander and his Adjutant, A. H. Baron Sloet van Oldruitenborgh. On July 15, the concept was submitted to the general assembly, with rules regarding ballot and acceptance of new members added. A proposal to have the Secretary frame minutes in accordance with the regulations was, though initially opposed, accepted. This obligation was confirmed in Article 16. We do not know what, if anything, the effect of this article was. In the following years the subject of Club regulations often resulted in a convivial meeting rather than a serious discussion. However, in 1843 a printed edition of briefly worded regulations appeared, containing sixteen articles. It was illustrated with baroque engravings by Rochussen. In the end Articles 12 and 13 contained definite directives for the ballot. In the following year, 1844, an English edition followed. After the death of Prince Alexander the stimulating and corrective forces of the presidency broke down. It then became clear, however, that strict regulations for gentlemen and falconers had become necessary. We must assume that during the meeting of June 25, 1849, the gentlemen got down to business. At long last, in 1850, the final version appeared nicely bound in a blue cover. It was signed by the Patron and President King William II. A supporting Commission was appointed: Prince Henry of the Netherlands; John Godolphin, Duke of Leeds; Edward Clough Newcome; E. L. Baron van Tuyll van Serooskerken van Vleuten and the Hon. H. Mollerus.

It is probably unique in the history of falconry that not only members of the Club but also their professional falconers were subjected to written regulations. It points to a certain perfectionism, but we must assume that it was not without reason. Unfortunately only one concept is known, the notes of which are conspicuous by their style. Apparently they were recorded by a clerk, whose calligraphy was better than his philology.

It took ten years, or in other words ten meetings, before definite regulations were drawn up and set out in detail. However, this was of no importance, since falcons needed no regulations to fly well and that was the only thing that mattered.

Button belonging to the official dress of the members of the Club. Gilted copper. The inscription reads "Mon Espoir est en Pennes," or "My hope lies in the wings."

Aigrette fastened in brooch with diamonds and semiprecious stones (1818–48).
Royal Collection.

Some articles need special attention. In Article 1, for instance, it is striking that originally one chief falconer is spoken of. In the following articles, two chieffalconers are mentioned. Could this mean that these regulations were drafted in 1840 when Mollen was not as yet in service? Or were they drawn up after the death of Prince Alexander when impending lack of funds and mounting financial difficulties led King William to think about employing only one falconer himself? It remains guesswork as to when and by whom the falconers' regulations were drafted. It could have been in 1848, since in that year for the first time and, alas, for the last, account of the flights was rendered, according to Article 6. In any case, the only trim and neatly bound account in the Royal House Archives is dated 1848.

Article 3 reads: "The Supervisory Committee shall be composed of 2 English and 3 Dutch Members, presided over by the Chairman." This shows the value given to the English members. Article 11 shows us that the gentlemen were seriously convinced of the necessity of a correct course of things. Not for nothing do we here again come across the names of two outstanding English falconers: "The Member of the Committee, charged with the control of personnel, has also to supervise the falconers, servants, falcons, etc... He must ensure that the material is kept in a proper state. And finally, during the stay at The Loo, he is to check the clothing of the falconers and other personnel and see that it is clean and well kept. During the season, the Duke of Leeds and Mr. Newcome, together with the member mentioned above, were to see that these articles were carried out."

In those days, clubs were the affairs of gentlemen, in whose vocabulary the word emancipation was missing. Article 14 clearly bears witness to this: "The Society shall be composed of Members and Honorary Members, whilst under no condition shall ladies be admitted to membership."

Everything was arranged down to the minutest details. The regulations even mentioned where subscriptions could be paid. For English members this was the banking house of S. Scott & Company, Cavendish Square, London. The Dutch, and probably the other foreign members, could meet their liabilities by payment to the current account of A. Baron Sirtema van Grovestins and, from 1848, to the account of Mr. Anemaet, Adj. Secretary to Prince Alexander. Anemaet was on friendly terms with Adriaan Mollen, as we shall see further on.

Was it perfection or wisdom that dictated that the respectable number of no less than five articles was dedicated to the admission of new members? Voting was secret and there was a small chest with two drawers bearing the inscription: Yes (Pour) and No (Contre).

Article 24 embodied the rules according to which the dress of the members was prescribed. The initial design of the members dress was as follows:

Design of dresses for Amazon and falconer used during the reign of the French King Louis XIII an enthusiastic falconer himself and the famous falconer—writer d'Arcussia (Arveuf, 1840). By Nicolaas Pieneman (1809-1894).
Royal Collection.

–A jacket of baize, fitted with the buttons of the Society.

–White breeches covering the boots for non-riding members.

–Boots black à l'Equière.

–Hat grey, fitted with an aigrette.

–Glove à la crispin for the left hand, plain brown for the right one.

–Falconer's bag green, fringed with gold braid.

–Cross belt of red leather, fringed with braid.

Members were not obliged to wear this uniform, but were invited to procure one as described. On studying illustrations of the Society and its members, it is clear that this invitation did not lead to the desired result. Each member retained his own dress but usually took care that it was in accordance with the distinguished style of falconry. The article concerning the use of horses was adhered to.

Article 25 describes the prerogative of the King regarding the award of the trophy to ladies: "It is only permitted to the Patron His Majesty the King and President, with prescience of The Committee, to grant the aigrette to a lady."

In the regulations of 1850, financial control was explicitly described. From the beginning, the falconers Bots and Mollen were not only responsible for the falcons but also for the personnel and the horses and their maintenance. This is evident from a note of expenses, destined for Prince Alexander and

Princes Sophie (1824–1897) arrives in the field in Fresian dress in a typical Fresian cart. By Nicolaas Pieneman (1809-1894).
Royal Collection.

paid by Mollen on July 9, 1842. The costs amounted to Dfl. 2812. 54[19], in those days no trifle. The Committee was obliged to meet these yearly charges from the contributions of the members. The balance-account of 1846 showed that payment was not too promptly made. Mollen remained in the red for the not inconsiderable sum of Dfl. 780. 92 and Bots for Dfl. 750. 171/2. More serious was the statement, added to the balance: "contributions not yet received Dfl. 1720 —." It is very understandable that the falconers were often in distress because of these overdue payments. The cause lay in the fact that many members were not really committed to the Haut Vol and found the costs underlying the pleasures of the Club too high. We shall elaborate on this subject later.

IV The Patronage of the House of Orange-Nassau

—Dedicated to the late Louise van Everdingen.

Three Orange rulers played a role in the history of the Hawking Club. [20] On October 9, 1838, King Willem I gave Messrs. Stuart Wortley and d'Offémont permission to practice, or rather, taste of the flight on the heron during the following season (1839). The King and his consort liked to stay at the Loo Palace, in contrast to the heir to the throne, Crown Prince Willem, who was born in 1792. While serving under the Duke of Wellington, he gained great renown on the battlefields of Spain and at Quatre Bras and Waterloo, which earned him the epithet of Hero of Waterloo. He coupled the art of warfare to a distinct feeling for the arts.

During the reign of his father, King Willem I, the Prince lived in England for quite some time, feeling very much at home in London society life. Although a very dynamic man, hunting did not mean much to him. When he succeeded to the throne in 1840 as King Willem II, his role in the Hawking Club therefore remained restricted to its patronage. Four children were born out of his marriage to the Russian Princess, Anna Paulowna: Crown Prince Willem (1870–90), the later King Willem III; Prince Alexander (1818–48); Prince Hendrik (1820–79) and Princess Sophie (1824–97).

King Willem II only ruled for a short period, from 1840 to 1849. It was his sons, the princes Willem and Alexander, who consolidated the existence and the glory of the Royal Dutch Hawking Club.

Traditionally, the relationship between father and eldest son, Willem, in the House of Orange was moderate to bad. It was the same here. Neither was prepared to move an inch towards the other. Willem was a difficult boy with entirely different interests to those of his father. He was pragmatic, more a man of deeds than of words. If he did not like something, he did not mince matters. His fits of temper were notorious. The Queen feared that the capricious and uncontrolled characteristics of his grandfather, Tsar Paul I, and his unstable grandmother, Sophie of Württemberg, recurred in the Crown Prince's character, making him unsuitable for the throne. Her hopes were pinned on the second son, Alexander, who, however, died in 1848.

Prince Alexander with a peregrine falcon. Watercolour by Jean Chrétien Valois (1809-94).

Instead of preparing himself for kingship, the Crown Prince lived the life of a bon vivant. He was fascinated by hunting and felt at home in the saddle. He was very artistic, a characteristic inherited from his parents. He loved the theatre and music, had a good baritone voice and could draw well. He was also interested in technique and made furniture as a hobby. He preferred life at the Loo Palace, with its uncomplicated and simple farmers, foresters, gamekeepers, and lumbermen to the stuffy atmosphere of the court, with its malicious intrigues and tensions. It was to be expected that such a pleasure-loving Crown Prince, with his aversion to the throne, would abdicate. His father had always kept him far from affairs of state. The Prince did not wish to take any responsibility for the impending liberalization of the constitution.

On June 18, 1839, Prince Willem and Princess Sophie of Württemberg were married in Württemberg, although she had given her heart to another. Willem and Sophie were first cousins, and it is understandable that Anna Paulowna was against the marriage. Apart from the circumstances surrounding the marriage, the contrasts between their characters were bound to result in disaster. Sophie had all that Willem lacked and did not recognize the good qualities he had. Where she was refined and erudite, Willem had no intellectual ambitions. He was often coarse and rude. Sophie had a thorough knowledge of affairs of state, politics, diplomacy and literature. Willem was hardly interested. Sophie liked good manners; Willem, however charming he could be, often disregarded them. Sophie had a well-developed social conscience. It took a disaster for Willem to show his. On the occasion of the floods in 1861, he was in his element, amongst his subjects and in the middle of dangers. In spite of all warnings, in rising water and drifting ice floes, he got into an unsteady little boat in order to encourage the rescue operations personally.

A year after the wedding, the marriage had already broken down completely and was no more than an administrative formality. The Crown Prince's children, the princes Willem and Maurits († 1850), were the source of many quarrels. On January 20, 1849, things came to a head and the Crown Prince left for England[21], not intending to return. However, within two months after his departure, the King became seriously ill. Everyone was thrown into confusion, not knowing where the Crown Prince was. King Willem II died on March 17. According to the constitution, he would automatically be succeeded by his son, but where was the new King, unaware of his kingship?

The ministers Lightenvelt and Donker Curtius, passionate hunters and horsemen and good friends of Willem III, immediately set off for England to look for him. They arrived just too late. Unaware of the events, Willem had left for Scotland to hunt. No one knew when he would return. The two ministers returned empty-handed and a new delegation was speedily dispatched, this time with more success. They were able to persuade the Crown Prince to accept the crown.

Crown Prince Willem was crowned[22] King Willem III on May 12, 1849.

The falconers company on the Soerense heath, Prince Alexander in the middle. Litho to Johann Sonderland by Johan Peter Berghaus (1810-70).
Royal Collection.

One must say that, up until then, he had been unpopular, but after his return from England his popularity increased. The people appreciated his uncomplicated character and natural charm. He got on well with ordinary people. In affairs of state, Willem proved to be more proficient than expected. He even turned out to be able to take advice.

His brother, Prince Alexander, was born on August 2, 1818 and was thus only a year younger than Willem. Since he was not to be King, Alexander's relationship with his father, obsessed by politics and statesmanship, was much better than that of Willem's. This is also apparent from the correspondence with his parents. The Prince was equable, friendly and courteous. His opinions were well-considered and never offended others. He got on very well with his older brother. Both were sporting and were excellent horsemen[23] and hunters. From their earliest days, they had spent many hours in the saddle in each other's company. Besides this, Alexander was an athlete and, with a view to riding, kept his weight under control. At the age of ten, they were already introduced to the secrets of horsemanship and later even had a race course laid out.

At the same time, their personal physician, Dr. Everard, himself a passionate hunter, made them familiar with shotgun and rifle. There is a letter from King Willem II to Prince Alexander, dated 1834, in which he urges cau-

Prince Alexander in clubattire with falcon glove and bag. Watercolour by Johann Sonderland.

Crownprince Willem, the future King Willem III, in the clubs attire. Watercolour by Johann Sonderland.

tion when the Prince goes with Everard from Soestdijk to hunt red deer on the Amersfoortse Berg and Hoge Klei.[24] In 1836, both princes visited England. They were accompanied by their father, then still Crown Prince, who had lived there for a long time. He was still fêted in London society as the hero of Waterloo and Quatre Bras. In 1838, Prince Alexander went to England again as the guest of the Duke of Leeds. The Duke and the Prince became good friends and a third visit followed in May, 1839. It is obvious that it was probably Prince Alexander who persuaded his grandfather, King Willem I, to give permission for the flight on the heron to be held at the Loo Palace in 1839 by way of a trial. Soon after the inauguration of the Royal Loo Hawking Club, the Prince became chairman and gave himself heart and soul to it. Once, when his presence was needed in The Hague during the hawking season, he wrote to his father:

> I long to remain at the Loo, where the flights this year are magnificent, better perhaps than they will be for a long time to come. You may disapprove of my behavior and my

King Willem III (1817-90) on horseback in the clubs attire. 1852, by Nicolaas Pieneman.

Queen Sophie (1818-77) holding a falcon, 1849, by Henri August d'Ainecy comte de Montpézat (1817-59).
Royal Collection.

decision but remember, dear father, that this is my only relaxation and the only pastime I really love.

Prince Alexander's great merit was that he invited artists such as Sonderland and Dubourcq[25] to record the activities at the Loo Palace. The famous ornithologist, Schlegel, and his huntingfriend, Verster van Wulverhorst, were called to the Loo Palace to see the hawks in their element. It is due to this initiative that we now have excellent reports on how the Club fared and are able to form a picture of the high flight on the heron.

Already during the most flourishing period of the Hawking Club, the Prince's health deteriorated and he was unable to stand any physical exertion. At the end of the Loo season, on July 21, 1847, the King received a letter from the Duke of Leeds, urgently requesting that their dear friend, Alexander, should be allowed to come to Scotland for his health and for the pleasures of the stag hunt. The King and Queen were most anxious and the journey fell through, he could no longer manage it. Chronic lung tuberculosis forced the Prince, desperately ill, to leave for Madeira on November 1, 1847.

Surrounded by the tender care of Doctor Everard and a few other faithful friends, the end came on the morning of February 20, 1848.

His untimely death, just before the '48 season, had an adverse effect on Club activities, in spite of the fact that Crown Prince Willem also heartily supported them. When eventually the costs began to run too high, he took on the entire burden of keeping one of the hawking teams himself in 1850. This was a costly business, which could not have come at a worse time, given the complex situation with regard to his father's heritage. Even when the Club was officially discontinued in 1855, Willem III attempted to carry on privately, a proof of his commitment.

While Prince Alexander was still alive, he had collected a circle of friends at the Loo Palace, called the Royal Loo House Club. Its membership largely overlapped that of the Hawking Club. These were men of leisure, who felt very much at home in outdoor life and within their circle of social equals. In the 1850s, however, the King's moodiness often tested the atmosphere of the meetings at the Loo Palace to such an extent that the guests decided to leave early. In her letters, Queen Sophie writes to her friend, Lady Malet[26], that only the Duke of Leeds remained, since he could not be insulted.

The importance Queen Sophie must have had for the Hawking Club is demonstrated by the portrait that H. A. Compte de Montpézat painted of her on a horse in 1849. She is the only member of the royal family to be portrayed with a hawk on her wrist, while her husband and brother-in-law only have a glove and a hawking bag. It is striking, however, that Queen Sophie never mentions hawking in her letters but refers to the pleasure that the fast horse rides give her. This could be explained by her short-sightedness, which made it impossible for her to watch the high flight. In any case, the presence of so many guests were a welcome interruption of her otherwise boring stay at the Loo Palace.

V The Falconers

—Dedicated to Steven Frank

It is not however the art of training and flying hunting-birds which stamps a person as a good falconer. To deserve this title he should posses other qualities. Above all things a falconer has to devote himself heart and soul to his trade. He must under no circumstances yield to vice. It is his duty to occupy himself with his birds and even with such care, that in case of emergency he will neglect his own well-being in favour of theirs. Incessantly he has to scrutinize his actions and invent a thousand and one tricks to solve any problem which might present itself. These tricks must be such that they can be put into practice in every individual case. Besides these qualities, the falconer must posses a constitution which enables him to resist fatigue. He should be patient in the face of every ordeal. He must be of a suppleness and flexibility of character so as to be able to associate with people of every social class!

—Schlegel and Verster van Wulverhorst

Through the ages, falconry was concentrated in the region called Kempen, situated on both sides of what is today the Dutch-Belgian border. The most significant centre was Valkenswaard, in earlier times called Verckenswaard.[27] The spacious surroundings of this village consisted of sandy soils and moors, in which several small fens could be found. In spring, these offered good breeding grounds for many bird species, and in the autumn they were frequented by migratory birds. Already at the end of August the first peregrines appeared. Here, from October 1, St. Bamis' Day, the falconers erected their simple turf huts,[28] surrounded by an intricate system of poles, lines, decoy birds and bownets. At a few yards distance from the hut a knoll was erected, on which the grey shrike was placed to warn them when a falcon came in sight.

At earliest dawn, after a stiff walk of an hour or more, the hawkcatchers sat down in their dark, damp and chilly huts to await the events of the day. It often took a long time before they could pull the line of the bownet. When they caught a falcon it was immediately hooded with a rufterhood[29] and put into a sock, so that it couldn't move and damage itself. Its talons were clipped, probably to prevent bumblefoot.[30] Once back home, the birds had to be cared for and tamed. This took many hours and the days were long and tiring. The falconers had no means of keeping the hawks' meat fresh for any length of time. Sometimes it had to be procured from the neighbourhood, for instance

Falconry party at The Loo, in the middle Queen Sophie, by Henri August d'Ainecy comte de Montpézat. Royal Collection.

the town of Eindhoven with its 3,000 inhabitants and only three butchers. The journey took two hours by foot but was probably more often made on horseback.

During the last three months of the year the huts were occupied for catching. According to information provided to Schlegel and Verster van Wulverhorst by Bots and Mollen, the first to appear were old falcons and tiercels, followed by young tiercels and finally young falcons. [31] As far as we know today, these were migrants from the north.

After the catching season, Bots and Mollen remained responsible for maintenance and training of the falcons in so far as this could be completed at Valkenswaard, in other words until the flights at kite and heron took place. Early in spring some falconers returned with their partly trained pupils to the royal courts in whose service they were. England, France, Germany and Portugal[32] were the most important. On the other hand, falconers from far away countries came to Valkenswaard to buy birds. This had to do with the fact that falconers, or rather hawk catchers, had united in companies and undertook long and hazardous travels to Iceland, Norway, Sweden and western Russia. They even penetrated into Kola Bay near present-day Moermansk to catch gyrfalcons. These were traded in Valkenswaard, if they were still of any value after these inclement travels, and sold to falconers from abroad or to falconers from Valkenswaard who had a tenure in those countries. Licences were issued by the Danish Kings, who ruled Iceland and great parts of Scandinavia. Men from Valkenswaard like Verhoeven en Verbruggen managed to gain a monopoly of catching and trading. Between 1731 and 1793, 4,649 gyrfalcons[33] from these countries were imported. One can understand that the enterprising catchers and falconers were rewarded for their dangerous travels and hardships by a certain prosperity.

The travels and the long stays at foreign courts and sometimes at distinguished clubs[34] gave them a veneer of education and well-bred manners. In Valkenswaard they belonged to the notables. This is apparent in their membership of the St. Catharina Guild,[35] a corporation of men of standing. In the regulations of this guild a clause was added to excuse absence from the yearly convention of the brotherhood, in the case of members being abroad for a longer period. It may safely be assumed that this clause was added on behalf of the falconers. Service abroad and the trade in gyrfalcons and peregrines brought them money, and salaries at The Loo were also several times higher than those a craftsman earned. Who were these enterprising men?

Frans van den Heuvel.

Frans van den Heuvel

It is probable that Frans van den Heuvel altered his Christian name during his French period. Though he had already left France forty years earlier, he signed a letter, dated July 18, 1840, in the French version. In England his Christian name was again altered to Frank. He was born in 1766 to Frans van den Heuvel and Johanna Maria van de Leur. Indeed the name van de Leur has been connected with "loer," meaning lure.[36] This could point to the fact that falconers' blood coursed through his veins from his mother's side too.

Frans Daams instructed him in the art in his early years. At the early age of fourteen years Frans left his parental home to enter the service of the Elector of Hessen-Kassel. After his death in 1785, Frans, now nineteen, moved to the falconry establishment at Versailles, where the Marquess de Forgès, Master of the Hunt to King Louis XVI, was in charge. Frans joined a good and familiar company: twelve falconers from his native village Valkenswaard, amongst whom members of the Daams family played an important and dominating role. He also met four colleagues from the village of Arendonk[37] situated in the vicinity of Valkenswaard. From his salary of 689 Fr. yearly[38], he could live comfortably, without however being eligible for a pension.

Ruth Botten, Frans van den Heuvel's wife.

Valkerij Museum Valkenswaard.

The royal falconry establishment in those years was past its best. Van den Heuvel was to serve the establishment for no more than two years because in 1787 the Marquess de Forgès informed the Danish King that the Haut Vol had to come to an end. Gyrfalcons, the traditional royal present, were no longer given after that year. Crow, magpie and partridge were flown at until this type of flight, not then very popular, definitely ceased in 1792. For a

Frans van den Heuvel (1766-1846). He was a falconer at the court of Versailles, in England and at The Loo. Bottom part of illustration: a cadge with hooded and bridled falcons. Watercolour by Johann Sonderland.
Royal Collection.

Chief falconer Jan Bots († 1864). He brought attention to falconry at The Loo grounds to the British High Ash Club. Watercolour by Johann Sonderland.
Royal Collection.

short time Frans returned to Valkenswaard. Later he entered the service of the Prince of Anhalt-Bernburg, where he remained for two years. Thereupon he became falconer to the Confederate Hawks of Great Britain and several members of this illustrious society. He married an English lady, Ruth Botten from Spoonhill. In 1828, already sixty-two years old, he returned to Valkenswaard to enjoy the pension granted to him by the descendants of Sir Robert Lawley in whose service he had been from 1804 to 1820. Like so many falconers from Valkenswaard, Frans was a striking personality, spoke several languages and was a master in the art of the Haut Vol. We assume that he readily complied with the request of acquaintances to support and honour the Haut Vol at The Loo with his presence. Alas, it was not to be for long. A letter from Jan Bots, dated February 3, 1846, read: "Thank God, we all are in good health except old Van den Heuvel who has a severe cold; my horses and Mollen's are in good health."

Shortly afterwards the old master died.

Chief falconer Adriaan Mollen mounts his horse and takes his position when the hawks arrive. Watercolour by Johann Sonderland.
Royal Collection.

Falconer Paul Bekkers (1815-59) kneels down when picking up a falcon. Watercolour by Johann Sonderland.
Royal Collection.

Jan Daems

The name of this falconer was also written Daams. He was born in 1744 in Valkenswaard to Hendrik Daems and Digna Bierens. Already an experienced falconer in 1772, Jan entered the service of Lord Orford. This gentleman was a member and probably the president of the Confederate Hawks of Great Britain, the society founded by Col. Thornton in that same year. This club, contrary to, for example, the Renfrewshire Subscription Hawks which practised the art of waiting[39] on, concentrated on the Haut Vol. Dutch falconers were invited and so the foundations were laid for sound cooperation, lasting a long time, in which Daems was one of the first to enter. Others joining successively were Bekkers and his sons Pieter and Jan; the brothers Pieter and Jan Lambert Danckers; Pieter Coppens; Pieter Weymans and Frans van den Heuvel, the latter in 1794. Moreover we find the names of the brothers Arnoud, Jacobus and Jan Bots and finally Jan Peels. Jan Daems and Frans Bekkers were the men who went yearly to Dovrefjell[40], Norway, to catch gyrfalcons. After delivering the hawks in England, Jan Daems could arrive just in time in Valkenswaard to man the hut for catching peregrines. He undertook this journey fifteen times, the sixteenth trip, in 1808, was to turn out differently.

En route from Valkenswaard to England the company of falconers, under direction of Daems, was in the The Hague to acquire passports for the passage to England. King Louis Napoleon[41], planning to restore falconry at The Loo, was warned by his secretary and had the company arrested.

Doubtless knowing the King's great interest in the sport, the secretary had no difficulty in preventing the issue of the passports. Maybe this arrest[42] was not unwelcome to Daems. He was now sixty-four years old and the tiring yearly journeys from England to Norway certainly did not make him long for more adventures. The King's offer made it possible to Daems to continue falconry in Holland without too much travelling. Be that as it may, Daems and his assistant falconer Jan Lambert Danckers left with ten falcons for The Loo. His pupil, Jan Peels, was sent to England with the hawks that remained. Lord Orford must have received him with mixed feeling, but Peels could not help it and had a valid excuse for his tutor Daems. The restoration of King Louis' falconry was, however, of short duration. In 1809 Daems returned to Valkenswaard, accompanied by some servants, helpers and thirty falcons, amongst them a few goshawks. Already in the following year the King was dismissed by his imperial brother Napoleon. What next?

Seven years later, in 1792 after the closing down of the royal falconry of the Elector of Hessen-Kassel in 1785, the activities at the court of Versailles came to an end. When the removal of Louis Napoleon from the Dutch throne by his brother Napoleon was effectuated in 1810, the last royal falconry practising the Haut Vol was a thing of the past.

In a letter[43] from the Chief Steward of the Royal Hunt, the Hon. Van Heeckeren, addressed to the Intendant General in Paris and dated August 18, 1810, the situation of falconers and Haut Vol was clearly explained:

> Finally I request Your Excellency to explain in Your report, intended for His Majesty the Emperor and King, that
>
> – the falconry establishment, being under my competency, is almost the only one in Europe,
>
> – the municipality of Valkenswaard, Department of the Rhine estuaries[44], from which I obtained my falconers, has been the meeting point and cradle of falconers to all reigning sovereigns through the ages,
>
> – it would be of importance to keep these men in Your service lest this institution gets lost,
>
> – I propose that His Majesty has them moved to Versailles or in case His Majesty does not attach importance to the continuation of falconry at the palace Het Loo in the

> province of Gelderland, where falconry is performed to the highest degree of perfection to any other place.

We do not know whether this letter was the only reason why Napoleon moved the falconers' company to Versailles. On August 2, 1810, the commander of the team at The Loo remarks:

> At last it has been determined that the establishment has to be transported. It is not yet known what measures have to be taken regarding falconry. Van Spengler will remain at The Loo until he receives further orders.

The date of both documents makes it clear that the removal took place after the end of the season. This meant that the flights in Versailles could only be continued in the spring and summer of 1811. Daems probably spent the autumn in Valkenswaard to catch and complete the preliminary training of the falcons. Actually falconry at Versailles did not amount to much. Only the lower standing flight at crow, magpie and partridge was practised. The royal Haut Vol therefore must be held to have ceased in 1810, to be followed forty-five years later by the Haut Vol in the context of a club, as we shall see. Since it was not possible to produce falcons in France, Daems yearly dispatched three of his men to Valkenswaard for the catch. The episode in Versailles was indeed of short duration. During these three years Napoleon only attended the flights twice. Daems was granted a pension and Napoleon presented him with a beautifully made falconer's bag. [45] It later came into the possession of his pupil, Jan Peels, who in turn gave it to his employer, the Duke of St. Albans, Hereditary Grand Falconer to the British Court.

After the French interlude Daems, then seventy years old, again went to England to practice the Haut Vol. Shortly before his death he returned to Valkenswaard, where he died at the high age of eighty-seven.

Jan Peels

Jan Peels was born in Valkenswaard around 1770. Already at the age of eleven he entered service as a falconer's assistant to the Elector of Hessen-Cassel. Soon he was charged with the care of the gyrfalcons, no small honour. Here Peels got ample opportunity to learn the tricks of flying the heron. After the death of the Elector his tenure ended, and he too left for England, probably in 1785, to enter the service of John Hall at Weston Colville. As usual, he went every year toValkenswaard to catch falcons. One can imagine that each summer, after the season, a real exodus of falconers from England to Valkenswaard took place.

As we have seen, the paths of Daems and Peels separated in 1808, when Daems left for The Loo. Taking with him some falcons, Peels continued the journey to England. These birds were probably destined for The Falconers' Club (Confederate Hawks of Great Britain) or for some participant members.

JE MAINTIENDRAI

Nous Jean Gisbert Baron Verstolk de Soelen, Chevalier Grand Croix de l'Ordre du Lion Belgique

Ministre d'Etat pour les Affaires Etrangeres de SA MAJESTE

Le Roi des Païs Bas, Prince d'Orange Nassau,

Grand Duc de Luxembourg &c. &c. &c.

Prions et Requérons

au nom de SA MAJESTE tous les Amiraux, Generaux, Gouverneurs, Commandans, Magistrats et autres Officiers, tant Civils que Militaires, quels qu'ils puissent être, des Princes et Etats, Amis et Alliés de SA MAJESTÉ, non seulement de laisser passer

avec ses Hardes et Bagages, allant à Vienne

sans lui donner ni souffrir, qu'il lui soit porté aucun trouble ou empêchement quelconque, mais aussi de lui donner ou faire donner au besoin toute aide et secours, ce que Nous serons prêts à reconnaître.

Donné à

sous l'empreinte de Nos Armes.

Signalement

Signes Particuliers

Valable pour un AN.

Signature du Porteur

A. Mollen

Lorsque le porteur se rend dans un endroit où réside un Ministre ou Agent Diplomatique du Roi, il sera obligé de faire viser son Passeport par le dit Ministre ou Agent Diplomatique.

Adriaan Mollen (1814-95) in uniform holding a hooded falcon. In 1938 the Nederlands Valkeniersverbond Adriaan Mollen was founded.

Museum Valkerij Valkenswaard.

Tearsheet from Adriaan Mollen's passport. It documents his trip to Vienna in 1838 when he worked for Prince Trautmansdorff.

Subsequently, he offered his services to Sir John Sebright and remained there till 1814. It is probable that he maintained his connections with the club, particularly with Col. Wilson, who took over the reins of this society in 1820. Until 1827, he went regularly to Valkenswaard to catch falcons. His next employment was in the service of the Duke of Leeds and finally he finished his career at the establishment of the Duke of St. Albans, where he started in 1832. In 1838 his son Jan was born. This Jan Peels went through life as John Pells. He succeeded his father in the service of the Duke of St. Albans and settled as a freelance falconer at Lakenheath after His Lordship gave up practising falconry. In 1845, he travelled to Iceland on an assignment for the Duke of Leeds and returned with fifteen gyrfalcons, eight of which were trained and stationed at The Loo. Neither Jan Peels nor his son John[46], who died in 1883, played an active role in the Royal Loo Hawking Club.

Jan Bots

On April 21, 1785, the falconers Gerardus Bots married Helena Coppens, descendant of a well-known falconer family. The marriage was blessed with sons, who were to follow their father's footsteps to England. Jan gained the most fame. He was a pupil of Jan Lambert Danckers, who accompanied said Daems to The Loo in 1808. After the fall of the French empire, Danckers and Daems found shelter at The Falconers' Club in 1821, Jan Bots coming with them. It was his first visit to England. Besides other acquaintances from his native village Valkenswaard, he there encountered his brother Jacobus.

As from 1829 his brother Arnoud also joined the company. Apparently he succeeded his brother Jan, who had the year before accepted employment at d'Offémont's estate in Compiègne, France. Bots introduced young Adriaan Mollen, fourteen years old as pupil and assistant falconer. In 1833[47], however, both left France and returned to England to serve The Falconers' Club. In 1838, the death of Lord Berners broke up this succesful society. Bots was appointed chief falconer of the Royal Loo Hawking Club then being formed. Adriaan Mollen, sufficiently experienced to act as his own master, entered the service of Prince Trautmannsdorf near Vienna. Arnoud Bots entered the service of the Royal Loo Hawking Club, acting as his brother's assistant. The third brother, Jacobus, established the Inn The Falcon (De Valk) at Valkenswaard (still existing).

From 1839 Jan Bots served the Club at The Loo with the greatest ability. He was the only falconer who attended the glorious flights on the Soeren moors from the very onset. He was the man who, after the termination of The Falconer's Club, pointed out the possibilities of The Loo. As such, maybe, he can be said to have been responsible for the origin of the Koninklijk Nederlandsch Valkeniers-Gezelschap, which became known internationally as the Royal Loo Hawking Club. It is therefore incomprehensible that Bots was dismissed without much ado when the activities at The Loo were declining.

Adriaan Mollen

This well-known falconer was born of the marriage of Johannes Hendrikus Mollen and Margaretha van Stratum in 1814. In 1833, young Adriaan left for England with his tutor Jan Bots to enter, at the request of Lord Berners, the service of The Falconers' Club. At the age of nineteen he had no doubt already mastered the noble art. Increasingly, this club had to overcome many hindrances. More and more grounds in the vicinity of Didlington were being put under cultivation and the Haut Vol became more and more difficult to follow on horseback. Lord Berners' death brought the club to a halt. We may assume that Mollen, after his stay in France, spoke the language reasonably well and that, after his stay at Didlington the English language did not present too many problems. He became acquainted with many adepts of falconry as, for instance, the Duke of Leeds, Stuart Wortley and Newcome. Afterwards, as we shall see, this would stand him in good stead.

In 1838 the paths of Bots and his pupil Mollen separated. The latter had in the meantime developed into an expert falconer, just like his tutor. He found employment at Prince Trautmannsdorf's estate in Oberwalsdorf near Vienna. His journey took nearly a month and was far from easy since he also had to care for falcons on the way. He also took charge of three sakerfalcons[48] from Hungary, two of them tiercels[49], for flying stone curlews[50].

Already in 1839, in the "experimental season," it became clear that Bots needed assistance, Van den Heuvel being too old to be of real help. Who could do better than the young, well-educated and experienced Mollen? A great problem arose in that he had only been in the service of Prince Trautmannsdorf for a very short time. The problem was put to Van den Heuvel and the old fox had good advice in store. He was all too well aware of the delicate character of his mission, knowing all the ins and outs of the Valkenswaard community. So he instructed a writer to send a strictly confidential letter to Mollen:

Dear Sir and Friend,

In the presence of Messrs. Newcome, d'Offémont and Wortley, the chief master of falconry, Tindal, from the Hague, ordered me to inform You that they would be pleased to have You entering their service as falconer and that they will secure You a good living, not only for one or two years, but for the rest of Your life. As You would have to inform Your present master, Prince Trautmannsdorf, Tindal and the other gentlemen will refrain from further action, unless the Prince is agreable. Please understand that under no circumstances would they wish to displease the Prince. If the Prince objects, please ask him in the name of these gentlemen if he would like to come to The Loo next season, accompanied by his falconers, to attend the flight at the heron for his own pleasure and that of others.

At The Loo this season we caught 113 herons; the birds did well, we lost a jerkin, the gyrfalcon caught some herons but started moulting early. I request You to reply soon, as I have to transmit Your answer to Tindal. Take care to keep all this a secret from Peels and all at Valkenswaard since I should dislike my part and that of the writter in this, to become known. Since it was too late, no excursion to Norway will be undertaken but we intend to go next season. Your family is in good health but they are ignorant about all this, nobody knows anything except me and the writer, so keep it secret.

Please answer soon. Your affectionate friend

Francis van den Heuvel

p. s. Both the young Princes were at The Loo and enjoyed the flights.

And so we see Mollen appear at The Loo in service of the Club in 1841.

This time he was not pupil and assistant falconer to Bots but a fully fledged chief falconer in his own right. Johan W. Peels succeeded him in Oberwalsdorf. Mollen was to go a long way and in the end became a Royal falconer, Bots, however, remaining in the service of the Club.

Already in the early days of the Club, a businesslike and friendly relationship had developed between Mollen and the well-known ornithologist Prof. Schlegel[51]. Soon, in 1842, Schlegel asked Mollen to let him have birds, skins and eggs. Mollen was able to provide these until 1861, but he then wrote to Schlegel, who in the meantime had become a good friend of his, to say that he would do better to address himself, through his mediation, to a certain Jasper, a bird catcher and poacher with an English clientele. Jasper, however, stopped his deliveries in 1863 because the English paid better and so Schlegel's business relations with Mollen came to an end. In the following year, 1864, the Old Hawking Club was founded in England. This meant more work for Mollen. In that year he had stood at the grave of his teacher Jan Bots and thus remained the only and last professional who mastered the art of the Haut Vol on the continent. Aided by his son and successor Karel, he caught and delivered twelve passage falcons to the club yearly. The Mollens also delivered birds in France, namely to Messrs. Pichot and Belvalette. The latter belonged to a younger generation than Pichot, and regularly visited Valkenswaard to learn the tricks of the trade from Mollen. In the year 1879, father and son Mollen had a very good catch: they pulled nineteen falcons under the bownet. Mollen stuffed birds as did his son Karel later. On November 4, 1889, the Zoological Society Natura Artis Magistra[52], got two peregrines from him and on October 10, 1890, he provided a gyrfalcon he had caught in the vicinity of the hamlet of Budel[53]. On July 27 the great master died and the tradition passed into the hands of his son, Karel Theodoor. Although he had never practised the flight on the heron, Karel was to be destined to be the last falcon catcher on the continent.

Jan Peels

In June, 1824, Johannes Wilhelmus Peels (called Jan) was born to the falconer Theodore Peels and his wife Joanna Catherine Feyen. Jan Peels, ancestor of the English branch of the Pells family, was his uncle. As with so many others, Jan imbibed falconry with his mother's milk. When The Loo tried to find an honorable way to have Mollen transfer to the Club, it was the eighteen-year-old Jan who aided the move by succeeeding Mollen at Prince Trautmannsdorf's. His stay was to be of short duration. Already in 1846 we find him on the wage list as assistant to Bots. When the Club expired in 1855, Peels was dismissed. A few years later, he succeeded Bekkers in the service of the Zoological Society Natura Artis Magistra (Amsterdam Zoo) caring for

Falconer Paul Mollen (1821-?), younger brother to Adriaan Mollen, as a cadgecarrier. Watercolour by Johann Sonderland.
Royal Collection.

Falconer Jan van den Boom handles a lure. Watercolour by Johann Sonderland.
Royal Collection.

the birds of prey. On November 12, 1896, he died and his son, in his turn, took his place.

PAUL MOLLEN

The fact that during his stay at The Loo, Paul Mollen earned less of a reputation than his well-known brother Adriaan, in whose service he was, could certainly not be ascribed to his abilities as a falconer. A service relationship between brothers is not by nature favourable. Maybe this situation influenced their personal relationship moreover, the difference in their ages may have contributed to Paul's modest role; he was born on May 10, 1821, and was thus seven years younger than his brother.

The pension, granted to Adriaan in 1859, did not apply to him. After a subordinate job at the Antwerp Zoo, fortune smiled at him and he could again practice falconry. He built another practice falconry, this time in the service of Lord Lilford. He built a hut to catch passage falcons himself, obtaining the remainder from his brother Adriaan. His knowledge of the Haut Vol was important to Paul in connection with the recently founded Old

An upbeat group of falconers and company. Left in front crownprince Willem, with riding whip. Watercolour by Johann Sonderland.
Royal Collction.

Hawking Club in England. It must be assumed that Newcome, who knew Paul very well from The Loo, was of help to him in gaining this position. The Old Hawking Club specialized in the flight at rook and crow as a replacement for the flight at the heron. Later on, the big aviaries of Lord Lilford also came under his supervision. The recognition he possibly lacked in Holland was lavishly bestowed on him in England. Lascelles (1899) did not disguise the fact that he learned quite a lot from him. His falcon, Bois le Duc, caught in the autumn of 1875, became famous—in its first season (1876), it killed no less than sixty rooks.

Peer Bekkers

Peer Bekkers stemmed from an old falconer family. In earlier centuries we already find the name Bekkers or Beckers. Frans Bekkers, in the service of The Falconers' Club, had two sons: Pieter and Jan. There is reason to assume that Pieter is the same as Peer Bekkers, who served the Club as second-in-command to Adriaan Mollen[54].

Jan van den Boom

Already in the eighteenth century, the family van den Boom had gained fame in falconry. We come across Jan van den Boom on the wage sheet of Bots, though on a lower scale. Probably he was assistant falconer rather than falconer.

In fact, the Koninklijk Nederlandsch Valkeniers-Gezelschap, soon called the Royal Loo Hawking Club, was a last resource for all these falconers. They flocked together from all points of the compass[55]: France, England and Austria, hardly having other means of existence. Their left hand was crooked by carrying the falcon, the right one commanded the delicate mechanics of hooding. It can not have escaped their notice that the existence of the Club, based on the delights of the Haut Vol, would be of only short duration. What was to be done? During their lifetime as falconers they had in some ways been comfortably off. The tiring and laborious travels to faraway courts were been thing of the past. Including the ferries over the Maas, Waal and Rhine Rivers, the journey from Valkenswaard to The Loo took at least two days. However, there were things in the organisation of the Club that could hardly have left the falconers unperturbed.

Both the chief falconers, Bots and Mollen, were fully responsible for their own personnel, falcons and horses. They had to pay the salaries to the former and care for the latter. If funds were scarce, they would obviously be tempted to make cuts in the salaries of their subordinates in order to maintain their own. Where Mollen, first from the Club and later from the King earned the generous wage of Dfl. 800, his subordinate, the falconer Bekkers, had to content himself with Dfl. 300 and Mollen's brother Paul with only Dfl. 280. Was the difference in workload as great as that? Doubt is justified. Bekkers was a first-class professional. With regards to Paul, later evidence proved him to be a falconer who mastered the art to the full. Furthermore, it is conspicuous that chief falconer Bots, Mollen's tutor and employed by the Club from the first, had to content himself with a wage of Dfl. 710, all in all Dfl. 80 less than his younger pupil. Bots in his turn paid Peels, before he succeeded Mollen at Prince Trautmannsdorf's, Dfl. 180.

Differences in rank and position within society as a whole were rigid in those days and obviously carried into the ranks of the falconers. Be that as it may, their abilities earned them the right to a place in the annals of falconry.

VI The Falcons

—Dedicated to the late Evert van de Beek.

The Peregrine Falcon

The peregrine's history is closely related to that of mankind. Deforestation[56] in earlier centuries enlarged its hunting grounds. Flat and spacious landscapes were conducive to the increase of its kind. From rocky coastal areas, richly populated by various bird species, it settled inland. Shortly after World War II this expansion almost became fatal, owing to encroaching cultivation and the increasing (mis)use of pesticides. In great parts of western Europe and North America[57] the peregrine nearly became extinct.

Except in Arctic regions, peregrines can be found everywhere there are bird populations of some importance. In its domain, the high sky, it rules supreme. Whatever tries to penetrate its territory, whether eagle, raven or crow, will soon learn to know the boundaries. In a playful and sometimes troublesome way, it will often meddle with other birds of prey, including trained falcons.

For the location of its eyrie the peregrine prefers a prominent ledge or the crevice of a rock. Where there are no rocks, for example on the tundra or in more southerly regions, dry hillocks will meet its requirements. In some parts of central Europe it will occupy or capture a nest built on a tree by some other bird, such as the crow or the black stork. It has even been known to chase the majestic sea eagle from its eyrie and take possession. Sometimes the peregrine is content with a high building, a spire[58] or even a large bridge. The highest known eyrie was situated at an altitude of nearly 4,000 metres. Anybody who wants to visit an eyrie must bear in mind that he will meet with furious resistance. The clutch of the falcon is not large, usually about three eggs. The mortality of young hawks in the first year is very high, approximately 70 percent.

Not everywhere in the world does this cosmopolitan have the same stature or the same attire. The transitions are gradual and the number of subspecies is small. There can be very distinct colour differences between nestlings and young falcons of the same eyrie: no two are ever alike. The purity of the various races was thrown into disorder by the fact that in captivity peregrines, and other falcons too, interbreed with falcons of different species, hunting habits and environment. Although there are faint rumours that hybridisation occurs in a natural environment, there is as yet no valid proof and it would in any case be extremely rare. This points to the fact that their mutual kinship is much closer than was ever expected. After leaving the eyrie the young hawks

The falcon Prince of Orange. She was the only falcon we know that was stabbed by a heron. Watercolour by Johann Sonderland.
Royal Collection.

remain for some months under their parents' care in order to learn their very specialized hunting techniques. If the food supply in the region of the eyrie remains good enough during autumn and winter, they are not inclined to migrate. The young falcons then try to occupy a territory in the same region or somewhat more to the south. If, however, climatic circumstances force their prey to migrate, then they too leave their native haunts, following their food supply. Birds from northern Europe are likely to occupy territories in regions where the climate of the gulfstream prevails, they may even travel far into Africa. North American peregrines are even said to migrate to Argentina. The peregrine is the incarnation of a cosmopolitan. There are few regions it cannot reach on its strong wings.

This falcon has hardly any natural foes. It is known that the eagle owl may, during the hours of twilight and darkness, incidentally kill a peregrine. Fox, raven and martin sometimes plunder accessible eyries. Man is its greatest

The falcon Sultan, portrayed with her owner Edward Clough Newcome.
Watercolour by Johann Sonderland.
Royal Collection.

enemy, robbing eggs or young and polluting its environment. Man is also its greatest friend. Countless generations of falconers loved and protected it and will continue to do so. It was the falconers whose initial breeding experiments opened the way to succesful repopulation[59] and so helped to prevent extinction of this highly endangered species in some regions.

The eyesight of falcons is legendary. Generally birds have a panoramic[60] field of vision and can thus see in front, to the side and partially behind them. Birds of prey, and falcons in particular, look straight ahead at the onlooker. In forward direction their vision is completely free. Like an awning, the supraorbital bone protects the eyes, but this is less accentuated in falcons and least of all in peregrines. The latter can see not only forwards, but also have a free field of vision upwards. Furthermore, birds of prey have a third eyelid, membrana nictitans, supposedly to enable them to look into concentrated light, as if through a grey filter. Their acuity[61] of vision is at least eight times that of

One of three gyrfalcons Prince Alexander donated to the Museum of Natural History in Leiden in 1842 and 1846.

man. He can observe a white spot like a tennis ball at a distance of 200 metres, but the eyes of the peregrine can cover approximately 1,600 metres. Their sight is predominantly black and white.

Beak

The beak consists of hard horn and is short and strongly curved. It partly covers the mandibula and has a protruding and pointed tip, so that it functions like a pair of scissors. A "tooth" behind the pointed tip is unique to the falcons, other birds of prey either lack it or show only a rudimentary one. If one connects the mandible joints with the tip of the beak a triangle with a narrow vertical angle is formed. Compared to other birds of prey, such as the eagle and buzzard, this angle is largest in the falcon, so that its beak is better for biting than for tearing. Falcons kill their prey by carefully exploring the cervical spinal cord and then breaking or dislocating one of the vertebrae. Intensive use of the beak encourages its growth, but a bird of prey will grind it on bones and rock surfaces in order to curb this.

Hands and Talons

Falconers speak of a peregrine's hands (fingers) and talons (claws). Though the musculature of the leg is strong, the fingers of the peregrine are too long to transmit great power to the talons. Peregrines "enclose" their prey, holding

Lithography by Joseph Wolf.
Bibliohtèque Centrale du Museum National d'Histoire Naturelle Paris

it effectively. For the kill, however, they depend chiefly on their strong beaks. Nearly all the other birds of prey, such as goshawks, for instance, have a stronger hand so that their talons can perforate and kill.

Stature

Peregrines are robust and stalwart. Of all falcons they are the most squat, stocky and compact[62]. Their plumage is suggestive of a polished surface, so that their air resistance is minimal. The primaries and tail feathers are resilient and able to withstand high pressure. This also gives them the ability to reach high speeds and change direction abruptly. The wings are long and pointed. The surface of wings and heavy body is relatively small, resulting in a high wingloading[63]. The energy consumption per kilometre is higher than that of birds of prey with a lower wingloading: eagle, buzzard and the harriers, for example, sail when looking for prey. The falcon has a somewhat "swept-back" wing. The aerodynamic faculties, which promote speed, are therefore enlarged. From observations, confirmed by scientific research, it has been deduced that a stooping peregrine can reach a speed of approximately 300 kilometres an hour[64].

Hunting Techniques

In the art of falconry various hunting techniques can be distinguished. Apart

Marmion, a peregrine falcon in juvenile plumage, a so-called 'red falcon' painted by Dubourcq, 1842.
Bibliothèque Centrale du Museum National d'Histoire Naturelle, Paris.

Will 'o the Wisp. By Dubourcq 1815-1873.
Bibliothèque Centrale du Museum National d'Histoire Naturelle, Paris.

Rocket gyrfalcon–tiercel–oilpainting (1842) By Dubourcq 1815-1873.
Bibliothèque Centrale du Museum National d'Histoire Naturelle, Paris.

Young Norwegian gyrfalcon on its prey, painted by J. Wolf.
Artis Bibliotheek Amsterdam.

from an adroit use of the force of gravity, falcons are expert in using the phenomenon of increasing windspeed in proportion to height above the earth's surface[65] to their advantage. If falcon and victim (e.g., pigeon or duck) maintain exactly the same airspeed in the same direction and downwind, and the falcon is flying higher, its groundspeed is greater than that of its lower flying victim. It will approach up to the moment in which the force of gravity can be used to stoop. When flying upwind, the opposite happens: the falcon is handicapped and the prey has the advantage. A great difference in height and a downwind direction of flight offer the falcon its best opportunities. The falcon's stoop often describes a parabole, given that it clutches after passing the deepest point of flight. So at the crucial moment, its final position of attack is behind and under its prey. The latter thus emerges from the camouflaging background and becomes clearly visible against the sky. Seen by a falcon with its predominantly black and white vision, the prey's silhouette gains in clarity and contrast and the pursuer can aim for the bull's eye. It is also possible that the prey's body increases the area of its own blind spot and that its wingbeats blur the field of vision behind it. This means that the falcon, attacking from behind, can be less accurately observed. At this point two things can occur: the falcon either slows down zigzagging and putting body, wings and tail into a position nearly perpendicular to its path of flight, enabling it to bind its prey and thereupon kill it on the ground. Alternatively, it may also maintain its speed or even increase it in order to mutilate or kill its prey solely by the impetus of the attack. Peregrines use both techniques separately or in combination.

The Art of Waiting On

After being unhooded and slipped, the falcon mounts in circles to an optimal height sometime before grouse or partridge, pointed[66] by the dog, is flushed. The position from which it attacks must be exactly timed to lead smoothly into the stoop, an art in itself. The dog is not allowed to point anything but grouse, pheasant or partridge and must ignore hare or rabbit in its path. Assistance from a beater or another dog is used to flush the game downwind. Waiting on is a difficult and complicated art: the start of the stoop is from a great height, the falconer and his dog having staged and prepared the scene, and the falcon takes over with its extremely spectacular flight and stoop.

Rook and Crow-Hawking

When flying these adroit birds, the falcon is slipped from the fist at the moment when they take wing. This can best be done at a distance of at least 100 metres or more, always upwing[67] enabling the falcon to mount more rapidly. Commotion and panic force the prey to decide whether to trust to its power of flight or to seek cover. The falcon in turn is forced to mount higher and higher and to stoop repeatedly until it can strike or blind its victim. Too often the latter, having evaded many stoops, is able to reach the safety of groundcover or trees. In this type of flight it is essential that from the beginning hawk and prey are approximately at the same level so that the former lacks the tactical advantage of waiting on.

The Haut Vol

This is an essentially different form of sport. Whereas they usually attack from above, in this case the falcons are required to start the attack from ground-level, their prey high-flying herons, which start to mount rapidly the moment they observe their foes below them. The falcon's task is to mount to the heron's level and subsequently surmount it, the greatest possible handicap. The Haut Vol can be said to be the reverse of waiting on, the latter providing an excellent starting position. The falcons are driven to the extreme and the magnificent peregrines in particular are capable of such a performance. These birdhunters par excellence and prima donnas of falconry were the life and soul of the establishment at The Loo.

THE GYRFALCON

Until now the gyrfalcon has not been able to push the peregrine off its lofty throne. In earlier times it was different. The appraisal of its robust and majestic stature was in no proportion to its actual ability as a hunting bird. The white Greenlander, clad in royal ermine, enjoyed the highest esteem.

Threatened by infectious and parasitic diseases, it rarely realised its full potential in warmer climates. Its stature differs from the peregrine's and is more in accordance with that of the falcons of the southern deserts, the saker and lanner[68]. Its prey is not numerous in its northern haunts. Unlike the peregrine, it is not entirely confined to birds as its build also enables it to catch small mammals. The wingloading is lower than that of the peregrine, as such it can fly and soar for a long time with a relatively low consumption of energy. The supraorbital ridge is somewhat more outspoken than that of the peregrine, so that intense light from above is of less hindrance when looking for prey on the ground. Whereas the peregrine has long aristocratic hands, those of the gyrfalcon are shorter and more robust, implying "handicraft." To smaller prey its clutch is deadly. The gyrfalcon's abilities are more diverse than those of the highly specialised peregrine. Apart from negative climatic influences great experience is needed in order to handle it as a hunting bird. Its character is often described as playful and untrustworthy, sometimes as obstinate. This falcon is strongly inclined to low surprise attacks in which goshawk and sparrowhawk excel. This method is alien to the peregrine. As we know from Mollen and Bots the gyrfalcons rarely met with succes. One of the greatest falconers[69] of our time wrote:

> The peregrine in this country can do all that these foreign hawks can do, and do it better. From time immemorial this has been the bird of falconry, the most universal and the most useful. It seems to have been created for the service of man. Its courage, docility, and the brilliance of its performance cannot be rivalled by any bird that flies.

An Icelandic gyrfalcon. Watercolour by Hermann Schlegel (1804-84), according to his comments, this was painted before he had seen a study by Joseph Wolf.

Icelandic gyrfalcon by Joseph Wolf. Watercolour study for a litho which is in the Traité de Fauconnerie.

Young peregrine tiercel. By Joseph Wolf.

Artis Bibliotheek Amsterdam.

Adult pergrine falcon, perched on an unusal place. By Joseph Wolf.
Valkerij en Sigarenmakerij Museum Valkenswaard.

VII Zoë

—A gyrfalcon from Dovrefjell, Norway, in service of the Royal Loo Hawking Club.

After the highlight of Haut Vol at The Loo one of the illustrations in *Traité de Fauconnerie* kept the remembrance of the glorious flights alive. The white falcon, *Faucon groënlandais*, fascinated falconers, bird painters and many lovers of nature. The composure of the bird is striking. To this day, the expression and beauty of this falcon represent the art of falconry in wide circles.

After World War II the Flemish falconer Charles Kruyfhooft, enthusiastic for the revival of falconry in the Low Countries, uttered his suspicion about the identity of the artist who painted the majestic and mysterious white falcon in *Traité de Fauconnerie*. Van de Wall entertained the same suspicion. Compared to other illustrations drawn by J. Wolf[I], the portrait of the white falcon is distinguished by the soft and delicate drawing of its plumage. The difference with other bird paintings is conspicuous; the pictures of the goshawks and other birds of prey generally show nervous and tense birds, feathers closed to their bodies. They are drawn along strict scientific patterns.

It is furthermore curious to observe that the pictures in the *Traité de Fauconnerie*, made on request of Schlegel, are often signed M. Wolf instead of J(oseph) Wolf, the talented painter we know already so well. M. probably for Monsieur. Our suspicions about the identity of the mysterious "lady in white" were sufficiently documented to stimulate further research.

In 1838 falconer Jan Bots from Valkenswaard and two devotees, Edward Clough Newcome and Vincent van Tuyll van Serooskerken, travelled to Dovrefjell in Norway to procure gyrfalcons. They returned with three young falcons. Newcome took one, maybe two falcons along to England. One remained in Holland.

In 1842 and 1846 Prince Alexander donated three gyrfalcons to the museum of Natural History of Leiden University, Director Prof. Hermann Schlegel. In 1842 at least one of those birds was three years old. Swaen (1863–1947) told that, as a young boy, he had lessons in drawing from Dubourcq (1815–1873). Before the war, in the thirties, van de Wall often visited Swaen in Amsterdam to study his collection of costly old books and prints pertaining to the art of falconry. One of these prints was a rough sketch in oil on cardboard of a young gyrfalcon named Zoë. Did Dubourcq himself present this falcon's portrait to his young pupil? And if so, was Swaen's interest in falconry and its history initiated by Dubourcq?

During the preparatory studies of falconry at The Loo, Piet Tuijn[II] discovered in the library of Leiden University some letters of Wolf, addressed to Schlegel. He dispatched the letters to van de Wall. Much to regret of the latter he could not decipher the intricate composition of the elaborate letters. He, however, had the good fortune that the wife of a colleague Mrs. Dr. Enklaar-Lagendijk, official of the German Institute of Utrecht University, was willing to "translate" them. Van de Wall was content to learn that his suspicion was correct and returned the translations to Tuijn, who on his turn sensed important historical items and started to follow the track meticulously. First of all, he detected the image of a Norwegian gyrfalcon, painted by Dubourcq in 1842. Tuijn:

> . . . The famous Wolf illustration of a white Gyrfalcon a gloved hand is the only plate by Wolf in the *Traité* dealing directly with falconry. The birds painted wearing hood and jesses. The other lithographs show birds of prey depicted in their natural surroundings without any falconry equipment. Without any doubt the *Groënlandais blanc mué*, as it is called in the book, is the best known and most reproduced plate of the *Traité*. It is often quoted as an example of Wolf's skill but, ironically, this plate is clearly based on a painting by Dubourcq and is now in the Fonds Pichot in Paris: "Zoé, Gerfaut agé de trois ans a pris 18 Herons au Loo, le 4 Juillet 1842 par Dubourcq" representing an adult gyrfalcon from Norway. In the same collection there is a lithograph after this painting, coloured by Wolf, as well as a pencil study by Wolf of a white gyrfalcon. On both these representations the position of the bird its hood and jesses are much like those depicted by Dubourcq. There are, however, important differences in length and outline of tail and wings between Dubourcq's painting and Wolf's pencil-drawing.
>
> Wolf's pencil-drawing might well have served as a model for his watercolour which was later owned by John Gould. It is signed and dated 1844. Some details of Wolf's pencil-drawing are more like those on the lithograph after Dubourcq's painting than those on the watercolour in the possesion of Gould and the lithograph in the Traité of the hood and in the position and length of the toes and talons of both of both feet this is obvious.

Tuijn accounts for the identity of Zoë in five points. The conclusion is clear and irrefutable: Dubourcq masterminded the white falcon and she moulted in Wolf's workshop from Norwegian silver-grey to Greenland white and she contributed distinctly to Wolf's fame.

Her effigy hung on the walls of the breakfast room in the Emperor's Crown and in the diningroom of the palace. We meet her in the book edition painted in the chilly and bleak-blue colours of her polar hunting ground. Obviously the background was altered on instruction of editor Arntz. Who made this lithograph in watercolour? Wolf? Palmer, Wolf's biography (1895) and others in their list of illustrations by Wolf mention that for the *Traité* as "autographs," meaning that Wolf lithographed his watercolours himself. This is probably not correct. Though Wolf had the ability to do the lithograph he

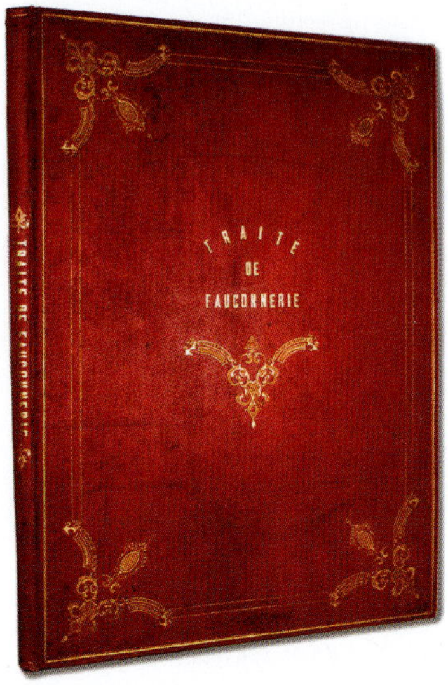

Cover of Traité de Fauconnerie in red leather, was bought by King William III.
Royal Collection.

The gyrfalcon Zoë sketched in oil. This portrait, in possession of Prof Swaen was done by Pierre Louis Dubourq (1815–73)
Bibliohtèque Centrale du Museum National d'Histoire Naturelle Paris

did not like this kind of work. As he stated in his letter to Schlegel of August, 14, 1843: "As you know I have said goodbye to lithography, which damages mind, breast and eyes."

In his letter of September 9, 1843, he mentions the possibility of lithographing the watercolours himself and he hastens to say that he still has to learn the special technique used for the *Traité*. Also in his letter of October 20, 1843, when discussing the various possibilities for "the finishing touch," he suggests that someone else will do the lithography. Schlegel, referring to the illustrations in the *Traité*, stated explicitly that they were lithographed by someone else.

While Zoë will live forever in falconers' dreams, the unknown person who made the last lithograph vanished forever in the polar night.

Zoë by J. Wolf, oil painting Dubourcq.

Bibliohtèque Centrale du Museum National d'Histoire Naturelle Paris.

VIII Training and Maintenance

—Dedicated to Henk Dijkstra

The first question put to falconers by laymen is always about the way in which falcons are trained. They know it is done but cannot understand that it is possible to let such wild birds fly freely and yet return to their owner.

Flying herons is a thing of the past. It is therefore difficult for the modern falconer to compare his own activities and results with those of his predecessors. The prey hunted in former times was not the birds' natural prey, whereas nowadays it is. This has reduced the handicap and, as far as the spectucular waiting on is concerned, has turned into an advantage for the falcon.

Training used to have obvious characteristics of force; nowadays subtle use is made of natural abilities. The principle is simple. The falcon is induced to substitute trust for its innate fear of man. It is this trust that forms the basis for letting the bird fly in complete freedom, with every chance of escaping, and return to the falconer.

In their introduction to the *Traité de Fauconnerie*, the authors thank the falconers Bots and Mollen for information, on the basis of which they were able to write the chapters on the daily care and training of hunting birds. This information was very detailed and, as such, unique. The works on falconry that had appeared up to that time had mainly drawn attention to all sorts of magic cures for real or imaginary ailments but training, daily care and flying for prey had hardly been touched upon. Bots and Mollen had a sane and healthy approach to their subject, as this extract from the *Traité de Fauconnerie* shows:

> The bad practices invented by oriental peoples, whose knowledge came to us in the tales and writings of Arabian falconers, have been completely discredited by modern falconers who are more enlightened than their forefathers and are guided solely by experience. They have reduced the art of keeping hunting birds to the most elementary facts. Recognising that there are no real and effective medicines for curing really sick birds, they therefore seek to prevent the illnesses rather than take useless measures to cure them, taking great pains to preserve the health of their birds.

Bots and Mollen realised the value of healthy and varied food. They well knew that pure protein, such as lean meat, eventually lowers weight and condition[70] and can therefore not be used for long periods at a time. They knew the importance of egg yolk, which contains everything a bird needs. They gave their falcons pigeon twice a week to provide them with sufficient calcium and other necessary elements of nourishment. This included feathers, necessary for the formation of castings[71]. Through observation they knew that birds in the wild do not, or cannot, kill every day. They used this knowledge, giving their birds a full crop on Saturdays and a half on Sundays. In this way they saw to it that Monday's flight could be made in optimal condition. According to them, gyrfalcons had a sluggish digestion. To keep them in good condition, it was necessary to give them full and half crops alternately.

They also deemed fresh air and regular baths of great importance. The bath was necessary in order to keep the plumage well groomed. Their attitude towards their birds—times have changed since then—was determined by their feats and was quite matter-of-fact. Only falcons with particularly good qualities or rare birds such as gyrfalcons had a claim to the mew. An unsatisfactory bird was at that time sent to the taxidermist or skin collector[72].

For sick birds with internal ailments they knew only one cure—freshly killed pigeon. They had an ingenious way of getting rid of lice and mites which came mostly from the food (pigeon and chicken).

Birds of prey are often bothered by lice. To get rid of these, make a brew of brandy and tobacco. After moistening the bird's head and neck, shoulders, tail and legs, the lice are smoked out and quickly die when they reach the moistened parts. One should have the assistance of two helpers during the first part of this operation, known as "washing the bird." One places the bird on a cushion on the table and holds it there, while the other, standing on the left, holds its talons. Two men are sufficient for the second part of the operation, "smoking the bird." One stands in front of the bird, which has been placed on the screenperch[73], the other behind. Using a clay pipe, the stem of which has been broken in half, light tobacco is placed in the bowl, covered by cakum and then lit. Putting the bowl in the mouth, smoke is blown through the stem that has been placed between the feathers.

As we have seen, everything was aimed at attaining optimal condition and preventing illness. With one or two birds this was practically feasible, but as soon as there were more daily care became half or even an entire day's work, to say nothing of the training itself. More must be said of this for a better undersanding of a falconers' work and its results, high above the heath of Soeren.

Schlegel and Verster van Wulverhorst were astonished when they first encountered falconry: "If one may call the art of training a dog for hunting a triumph of man over beast, that of training birds for the same goal is one which must in the first instance give rise to even more astonishment."

In contrast to the training methods used today, training in those days was an extremely lengthy and time-consuming business, taking into account that the falcons were expected to strike large, unnatural prey. They also had to fly in couples which is not their usual method. Last but not least, the falcons

The falconroom with perches for the falcons. On the left from the fireplace are the cadges, and on the right the falconbags. Watercolour by Johann Sonderland.
Royal Collection.

were confronted with a serious handicap; starting from the first, they had to rise above an ascending prey in order to attain an advantageous position for the attack.

According to the authors of the *Traité de Fauconnerie*, training in those days was based on force, induced by hunger and a healthy appetite. Real hunger greatly undermines the health of the valuable birds. A good appetite, however, serves to convince them that a deal can be made with the falconer. Bots and Mollen stimulated the appetite by means of physical exertion. This was done by carrying the birds on the first for at least two hours twice daily. To this end, recently captured wild birds were even carried from four o'clock in the afternoon until eleven o'clock at night. Another reason for this was to encourage subjection by means of fatigue. The art was to get the falcon to feed from the fist the day after being caught. Adriaan Mollen boasted that he could feed a falcon a quarter of a crop more than other falconers[74].

In the courtyard the falcons are brought outside on cadges, and then carried to the heath. In the middle is a self-portrait of Sonderland. Watercolour by Johann Sonderland. Royal Collection.

Training would be unthinkable without the hood[75]. This accessory is indispensable for letting the falcon become accustomed to man and his surroundings. It eliminates the all-important element of sight and puts the bird into a state of absolute subjection, dependance and repose. Getting used to man may take anywhere from one to several days.

The hood is also needed for transport on the fist or cadge[76]. Without it, the falcon might at any moment see prey and take flight or be otherwise disturbed. As soon as a passage hawk remains relaxed when standing on fist, it is unhooded in quiet, fairly dark surroundings and hooded again at the slightest sign of restlessness or panic. The intervals between unhooding and hooding are gradually increased in frequency and length according to the ease with which the bird accepts its surroundings. Finally, the hood is only used for transport.

Before looking at the training of passage hawks for the Haut Vol, a few

During the training. Drawings by Johann Sonderland.

words on flying at hack[77] and waiting on[78]. Both Bots and Mollen learned of the former in England, as is obvious from the very lengthy and detailed description of the technique by Schlegel and Verster van Wulverhorst. It was definitely not practiced at The Loo. Members of the Club could have brought eyasses back from England in the summer but there was another reason, namely, hacking takes place during the heron season and the disturbance which young birds in free flight would have caused by taking part in the tournaments in their own way was the last thing its members wanted. Although Prince Alexander was a great lover of falcon and pointer[79], the ideal combination for waiting on, this spectacular branch of falconry was never practiced in the Netherlands in the nineteenth century.

The passage falcons were given an extremely thorough training with endless repetition at each stage. Step by step they grew accustomed to man and his surroundings. They were carried for hours, morning and evening, before the lessons were given in a room. In order to accustom the bird to being

touched, it was stroked with a pigeon wing or twig. As soon as the birds fed unhooded, after about eight days, they were encouraged to jump onto the fist from the screenperch or the back of a chair. This was repeated four or five times a day and the last time the bird was fed a full crop. However good the progress, carrying continued morning and evening. It was even advised to continue doing this during the entire season. Within two to three weeks, the distance the bird was required to cover when called was increased to the entire length of the room. The whole exercise was then repeated out of doors for a similar period. It was intended to strenghten the relationship of trust between bird and man so that the falcon would always return to the falconer instead of taking to flight or fleeing.

The next stage, indoors again, was to show the falcon a live pigeon on a creance[80] which was gradually lengthened over a period of two to three weeks. When the falcon had got used to the pigeon, this was replaced, first by a chicken and then a cockerel[81], well able to defend itself and thus making great demands on the falcon. It could take from two to six weeks before the falcon

Necessary accessories for training and for hunting: hoods, lures and bags. J.Wolf. Traité de Fauconnerie.
Valkerij en Sigarenmakerij Museum Valkenswaard.

IX

N
the pe
the fis
These
trifle c
enjoye
expans
the vas
The V
west b
bogs. I
east by
Zuider
outer r
Zuider
vast m
The
and oc
The L
left pr
moder
local sl
The
tive. E
turf hu
more t
sheep.
dunes
In t

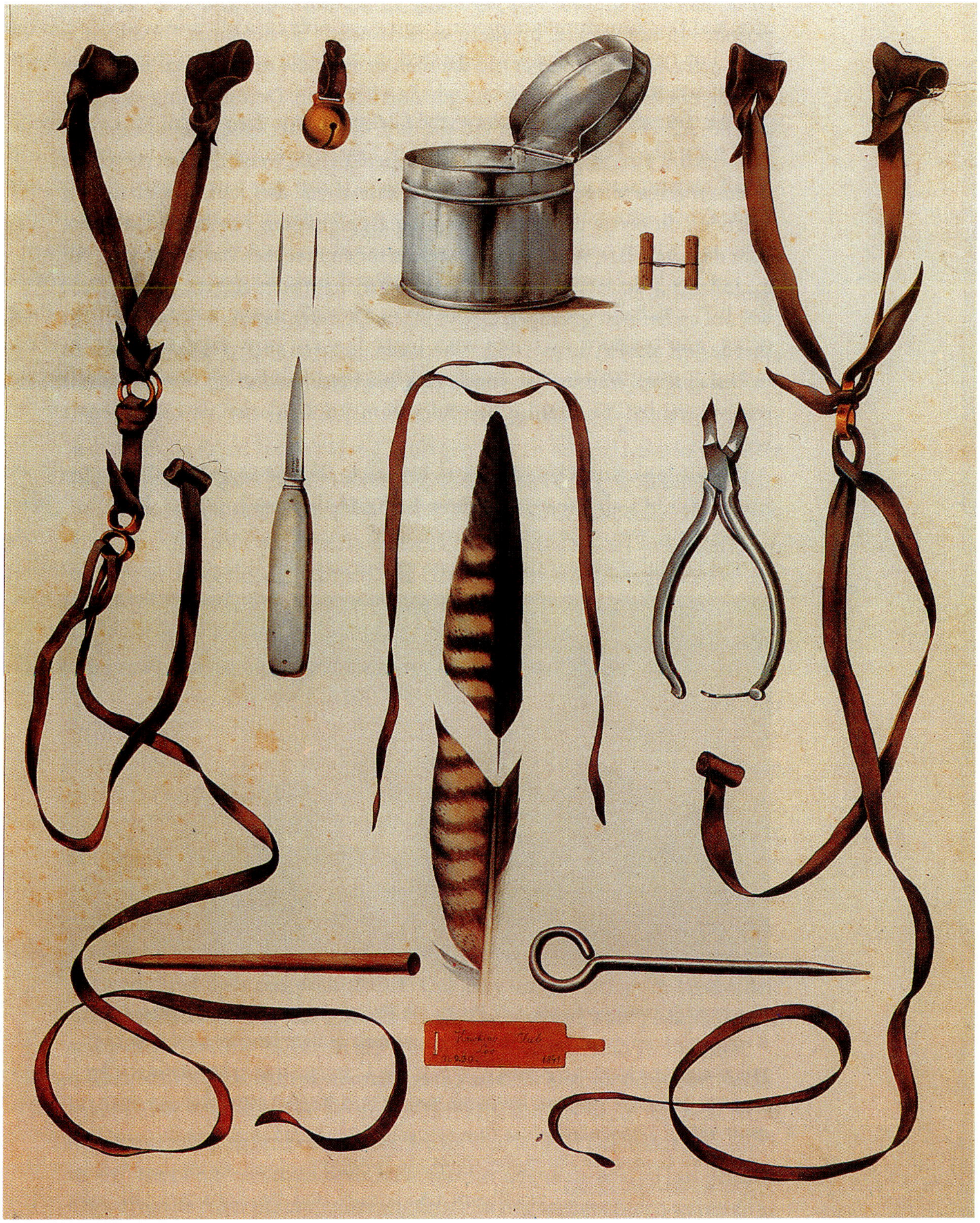

Also, a long leather leash, a short leash, needles for repairing broken feathers, a bell and other equipment .
J. Wolf. Traité de Fauconnerie.
Valkerij en Sigarenmakerij Museum Valkenswaard.

In the courtyard of the Emperor's Crown Inn before departing. Left, Baron and Baronesse van Verschuer. In the background, in the window of the first floor, the painter Dubourcq. At far right the guard: J. Van Engelen. Watercolour by Johann Sonderland. *Royal Collection.*

in the area and started cultivation. This had become possible since a law, allowing individuals to sell, promoted the claiming of grounds for agricultural purposes. In the second half of the century clippers imported guano and so the poorest soil began to bear fruit. The grandeur of the scenery diminished as the horizon narrowed. Today one needs a great deal of imagination to reconstruct the landscape of that time from old maps. Until far into the nineteenth century horse and coach were the only means of transport. Even Apeldoorn, the Royal residence, had not yet been connected to the west by rail.

This town arose on the higher eastern fringe of the Veluwe, well protected from the yearly inundations caused by the Ijssel River. To the northeast and less than half an hour by foot was the Royal Palace *Het Loo* and nearby the much smaller castle *Oude Loo*, stemming from the middle ages. By buying it from the Dutch branch of the Bentinck family, it came into possession of the Orange-Nassau sovereigns. Not long afterwards, in 1685, King-Stadt-holder

The Royal Family is departing. Left, the The Anchor Inn, right the Posthouse.
Watercolour by Johann Sonderland.
Royal Collection.

William III erected the beautiful palace *Het Loo*. This allowed him to take advantage of the estate for hunting big game with hounds and falconry.

At the beginning of the last century, members of the club could stay in the Groot Logement (Big Inn) situated on the eastern part of the avenue at the front of the palace, which had in earlier times lead to the highway to the town of Zwolle. It was here that the Duke and Duchess of Leeds entertained other members and guests for dinner. A room in the inn was adapted to house the falcons. In 1868 the establishment was sold and demolished. One could also stay at the Emperor's Crown (Hotel de Keizerskroon), an inn adjacent to the palace and dating from 1689. Opposite this inn were stables as well as a room for the falcons. Newcome used to stay at The New Crown (de Nieuwe Kroon), erected in 1843 at the beginning of The Loo Avenue. Both hotels still exist today, be it not in the original buildings, the latter under the name of Hotel Bloemink. Newcome enjoyed the advantage of keeping four falcons under his own personal care, choosing their company and smoking his pipe at leisure. After the death of King William II, Newcome and his wife stayed at the Old Loo as guests of Prince Alexander. If convenient, guests could be lodged at the palace. Between the Emperor's Crown and the palace garden was the Old Posthouse, which also had accomodation for horses and falcons.

From the palace a long avenue, called the King's Avenue, led through shady woods in Westerly direction for approximately five kilometres to the Soeren Heath. Nearly halfway there was a deep well, called The Echoput, near a small inn, still existing today but now a first-class hotel under the same name. From here one could proceed to the Soeren Heath or turn north to the Wiesel Heath, both ideal plains for witnessing the flights, the direction of the wind dictating where the society should meet. Both were situated north of the highway connecting Apeldoorn with Voorthuizen and, farther west, the town of Amersfoort. In some places sheds had been erected and there the New Crown offered refreshments. In case of unfavourable weather they served as shelters. South of the highway were the Soeren woods that grew on a swampy substratum with small ponds. Herons had been here for centuries and thus induced to found a very large colony for falconry. In earlier times the forest was called Reigerskooi (Heron's Cage) later on Reigersbos (Heron's Wood). Today it is known under the latter name, and the stumps of the nesting trees can still be seen.

If it was fine summer weather one could, after a quiet breakfast, settle in the shade of the lime trees in front of the New Crown and pore over the morning post or the daily newspaper. Besides the Dutch papers, *The Times* and *The Globe* were also delivered so that the English members could study the stock market reports. One could also watch the falconers busy with their birds. These had to be moved from the screenperches indoors to weather on the blocks in the open air. Some had to be given a bath and others had to be carried on fist. Jesses, swivels and leashes had to be checked and replaced if necessary. "Washing and smoking" of a mite-infected falcon was time-consuming. In short the falconers were very busy: "All day long the falconers were busy walking with hooded falcons by turns on the left wrist. To tame them they caressed the birds with the wing of a pigeon. [85]"

A letter of Prince Alexander to his father King William II dated June 19, 1840, contains fragments which provide us with valuable and interesting information: "The mornings are spent fishing, target-shooting and attending the training of cormorants[86] and young falcons[87] which is very entertaining and amusing."

The prince, and no doubt others, enjoyed the early morning hours stalking roebuck in the grounds surrounding the palace where these beautiful and graceful animals had their haunts: "On Wednesday morning I awaited roedeer in vain."

A fervent dog lover, particularly of pointers, the Prince liked to go out with

Falconry scenes.
Drawings by Pierre Dubourcq.
Royal Collection.

Newcome. He noted: "We had a "duck hunt" and it was very amusing to observe the efforts of the duck and Mr. Newcome's excellent New Foundlander.[88]"

The morning hours were quite demanding, all this alternating with visiting the stables and exercising the horses. It is clear that, providing that the previous evening's dinner had not been too copious, the club members could be very pleasantly occupied.

By afternoon the falconers had hooded the hawks and placed them on the cadges. Some restless birds were brailed before moving off. The daily carrying of the heavy cadges to the fields of Soeren and Wiesel must have been heavy labour for falconers and aides. In the shady King's Avenue it was not so uncomfortable but on the open heath the sun could burn mercilessly. They departed earlier than the mounted company so as to be present at around four o'clock. After arrival on the flat and gently sloping plain everyone went to one of the sheds, suchas the one on Falcon's Hill, to await the coming events. Onlookers from the Soeren or Wiesel hamlets had also gathered in the meantime. For the children especially it was a big feast. They gaped in admiration at the beautiful masquerade costumes[89] of the falconers and knew all to well that the distinguished company was liberal in distributing coins ot organizing the games which the young people loved. They valued it highly and found it worthwhile to walk the long distance from their home to the meeting.

In June and July the dominating wind varied from southwest to southeast.

Having foraged along the borders of the Zuiderzee, the Ijssel River and Lake Uddel, the herons were forced to fly upwind to their nests and young in the Reigerskooi. In a strong wind they chose the line of least resistance and flew low. This in itself did not greatly hamper the flight but the show was far from beautiful. It meant Haut Vol at low level. Moreover it could happen only too easily that the whole chase went downwind at high speed, soon taking falcons and herons out of sight. A moderate headwind alternating with periods of calm offered the best flights. From the start the herons were "lying high," and from the moment they sighted the peregrines deep below, they immediately started to mount even higher. This manoeuvre greatly increased the handicap for the falcons. At this point it was no longer of interest whether the falcons would succeed in bringing down the heron. What mattered was the sheer beauty of the flight.

Mounting aircurrents, changes in the direction of the wind and the condition of falcons and heron made for uniqueness of each flight.

If the flight failed, a falcon often directed his agression to other birds such as crows or pigeons. Probably it was usually crows that suffered and were sometimes even killed because they often interfered in the proceedings, cawing harshly. If they disturbed the concentration of the falcons the latter sometimes started in pursuit. In such cases the falconers were obliged to follow the flight on horseback to prevent the loss of the falcon. They did not always manage to get the bird on fist the same day as we can read in Jan Bots' diary of June 5, 1843: "Seen in the Newspaper of Arnhem of the 5th an announcement that at Rheden Mr. J. C. Bank, baker, has caught a trained falcon. I drove over and found the falcon *Black Prince* in tolerable condition."

À la Vol

Around four o'clock everything was ready. The force and direction of the wind were favourable and the sky was lightly clouded so that the silhouettes of the combatants would be clear, in contrast to the blinding effect of a cloudless blue sky. Expectations were high. The falcons had been moved from the cadges to the ground where they were fastened by leashes and pins. In the meantime, one of the assistant falconers on horseback took position approximately one kilometre downwind. From this point he could well observe the oncoming herons from afar. As soon as he saw the first one approach he dismounted and turned the horse in the direction of the approaching herons. At this signal two falconers went a few hundred metres in the direction of the heronry. Dependent on weather conditions, the starting point had been chosen two to eight kilometres away from the heronry. The heron was allowed to pass over for a few hundred metres before the falcons were

The Duke of Leeds in falconers outfit.
Watercolour by Johann Sonderland. Royal Collection.

Edward Newcome in action, preparatory study.
Watercolour by Johann Sonderland. Royal Collection.

unhooded and slipped. At this moment the participants cried "À la Vol" and the tournament had begun.

The falcons, in this case *Napoleon* and *Blücher*, had to deal with a vigorous handicap. The heron "lay high" and the falcons had to mount from ground level to a position favourable to opening the attack. The heron had the choice of mounting or trying to reach the heronry where the trees promised safety. As if not in the least motivated, *Napoleon* flew low downwind and was soon out of sight. *Blücher*, on the other hand, initially stayed low for a few moments, then mounted with strong wingbeats until a promising position was gained between the heronry and the waylaid heron. The latter became confused, gave up his original plan and started to mount in circles. These tactics forced *Blücher* to mount more quickly. In narrow circles the falcon worked its way higher and higher, intent on keeping the heron downwind as much as possible. His climb was laborious, and every gust of wind, however small, was immediately exploited to gain more height. In the meantime the mounted company had dispersed, each to the spot where he thought the heron would come down. It was as yet impossible to predict which of the combatants would be victorious. It was not even certain that the flight would be succesful. *Blücher* had to face battle alone, *Napoleon* as yet not visible, his actions inscrutable. *Blücher* managed to gain position above the heron, from where he could stoop with tremendous speed. The heron in its turn was able to evade the thrust, manoeuvring with lighting speed, too quickly to give the falcon a chance to change direction at the last moment. *Blücher* again had to prove his strength and endurance by surmounting the climbing heron to a new position from whence he could attack. The riders, far beneath the scene or battle, kept on guessing and turning their horses. Painstakingly they kept the movements of the experienced falconers in sight. Suddenly one of them called out "*Napoleon*!" but not all saw him. A mere speck, quickly growing larger, this falcon sped like a meteor through the sky high above *Blücher* and the heron which was fighting for its life. With folded wings *Napoleon* struck and was able to deliver the first blow to the heron, which had concentrated on *Blücher*. A moment later, not yet recovered from its fright, the heron had to take its second beating from *Blücher*, stooping in turn. The falcons, self-confident and encouraged by their success, did not leave off. Alternately, they stooped and mounted until *Blücher* dealt the last blow and bound the heron, on which both tumbled down. *Napoleon* was called to the lure, fed, hooded and replaced on the cadge. *Blücher* was taken off the heron on a pigeon's wing. The latter had lost his aigrette to the rider who had first arrived at the scene, was banded and subsequently allowed to go his own way.

These were the flights about which Prince Alexander wrote in the letter mentioned above:

> We were not favoured by good weather, the wind was strong and it was pouring with rain. So we were forced to fly the falcons very late. I hope that next week will bring us more favourable weather....
>
> The evening of my arrival we caught some herons with the falcons, it was superb to witness. The last heron defended itself gallantly and caused the falcons much trouble. It was a beautiful flight. Next morning the wind was too strong. In the evening, however, it grew less and we could fly the falcons succesfully.
>
> Yesterday evening we could not start before eight o'clock because of rain and wind; today it is still raining. It is now six o'clock and still raining but we shall wait till sunset. Falconry is worth watching and it is very interesting to see how the falcons are trained. The falconers are dressed in uniforms resembling those of the times of King Louis XIII of France; they are very attractive and simple. Those present at this moment are: The Duke of Leeds, Mr. Worthley and his wife, two Messrs. Newcome, Baron d'Offémont, Count Ranzow, Mr. Jerningham and Mr. Tindal. Mr. Jan Dedel left us yesterday morning.

The King and Queen Anna Paulowna will have enjoyed this letter from their favourite and beloved son whose health at the time was already precarious and caused serious anxiety.

We have seen that the flight did not always go easily and smoothly: weather conditions and interference by crows, for example, could not be controlled. Neither could the condition and motivation of the hawks always clearly be ascertained. This was determined not only by the hawk's behaviour but also by palpation of the breast musculature. However experienced one was, the opinion was subjective. Scales[90] had not yet been introduced in falconry. Just how difficult it was is illustrated by the journal entires of the chief falconers Bots and Mollen. The following is derived from Bots' register, dealing with the period May 1 to July 12.

74 herons caught.

May 10th – by *Duke of Wellington* and *Black Prince*; beautiful flight but nothing caught.

May 24th – Unhooded and slipped at heron, crows hindered, have caught one of them.

June 5th – The advertisement in the *Arnhem Newspaper*, earlier mentioned.

June 8th – Extremely beautiful flight, both falcons working very well to attack the heron, but in the end the heron outmastered the falcons.

June 11th – One heron bound in the Soeren wood but it freed itself.

June 17th – Caught nothing, the heron fleeing in the Soeren wood and the falcons not able to attack. Caught a crow.

June 18th – The falcons crabbed, the heron freed itself.

Junbe 24th-25th – This afternoon 24th a heavy thunderstorm and rain hindered us, no catch. Rain prevented our going out.

June 29th – The falcons gave up, the heron lying too high, the falcons abandoned it.

For the 1844 season Mollen noted as follows: two hawks were always flown. Names: *Prince Albert*, *Marnix*, *Empereur*, *Dauntlesse*, *Napoleon*, *Blücher*, *de Ruyter*, *Bulldog*, *Thunderbolt*.

May 24th – At Assel: caught a heron banded in 1843.

June 10th – At Wiesel: lost *Royale*, recovered in the morning.

June 19th – Flew with *Napoleon* and *Blücher*; lost *Napoleon*, recovered on the 20th, heron caught in the shrubs.

June 29th – *Napoleon* and *Sultan* caught a heron banded in 1843.

July 2nd – *Dart* and *De Ruyter*: caught a crow with *Bulldog*.

Total from May 4th – July 12th 80 herons.

These are but a few data, however, they clearly show that the proceedings were not always that easy and that the Haut Vol could often be characterized as a game of hazard.

Back to the company, which, after the flight of *Napoleon* and *Blücher* met again in expectation of the performance of the next team of hawks. In the meantime it had grown later and the wind had dropped. Quite soon the lookout signalled herons coming. Sharp eyes saw him pointing upwards, signifying that they were "lying high." And so it was—the heron was tracking at great height in the direction of the heronry when both hawks were slipped. The position of the heron was advantageous, it could probably reach safety before the threatening hawks had surmounted it. The latter had the disadvantage of lack of wind which made their climbing more laborious since they could not exploit headwind lift. The falconers had taken this into full account and had consequently slipped the falcons before the heron had passed them. It was an excellent team cooperating superbly. Both hawks were persevering and ready to do their utmost to catch their heron, which began to mount in spirals. The show was breathtaking and thrilling. Meanwhile the falcons were so high that they could only be seen as mere specks. Nobody had as yet seen them stooping. The heron defended itself stubbornly by climbing higher and higher. The tension was palpable: who would win? Would the falcons persevere? The first stoop was observed but was evaded by the heron, costing it precious height and ultimately sealing its fate. Like lightning it had to evade the second falcon, costing it more precious height. Five more times the falcons had to mount to strike succesfully. Then the heron gave up, and like a big ball the hawks and their prey tumbled down to earth.

And then, all of a sudden, there they were—crows! Inquisitive and loudly cawing and protesting, they began to interfere. In a moment of flaring agression one of the falcons dropped the heron and without hesitation attacked in hot pursuit. One of the tribe was moulting badly and had to take the full brunt of the assault. From a safe distance the rest of thecrow brotherhood followed the battle, ready to interfere at any moment. The falconers immediately saw the danger. One of them started to follow the flight on horseback.

In a straight line the crow, hardly hampered by his retarded moult, made for the woods near Lake Uddel. The falcon having shortly before spent much energy, followed him laboriously. Once above the trees the crow dropped like a stone and was able to save itself. The falcon however was lucky. Far below, on their way to the lake, duck fled and the raptor managed to bind one in the first stoop. Plucking its prey and relishing the fat neck, it was far out of sight of the falconer who, after a fruitless search, rode back to the company. Twilight was coming. Meanwhile, the other falcon was taken from the heron and had taken place on the fist. The prize was thoroughly inspected. One of the falconers had fixed it between his knees and had stripped off the aigrette. The crop had already been emptied of fish[91] during the pursuit in order to be able to mount more quickly. Along neck and back, long scratches showed. Subsequently it was hooded and its dangerous beak rendered harmless by means of a tube of elder. Then it was taken away to serve in the training of the less experienced hawks, for example those caught late in the season.

Peregrine falcon on heron. We may safely assume that Edward Newcome stuffed this bird. At present this beautiful preparation can be admired in the Aardhuis, former shooting lodge of King William III. It is the most precious reliquary in the history of falconry.

In the meantime, the lost falcon had chosen a comfortable roosting place in which to spend the night. While basking itself in the warmth of the rising sun and pluming its feathers, it observed a lone rider on a ridge of drift sands who dismounted and swung the lure. But the duck's neck was a copious meal and the falcon had not as yet thrown its casting. Why bother about a lure? Scratching the nape of its neck with one leg, its bell jingled loudly. The falconer, however, was too far away to hear it. Some time elapsed before the falcon took wing again. Had it failed the duck the evening before, it would probably have accepted the lure. Some days later it observed a sportsman who was shooting partridge in the company of his pointer. Adroitly, the falcon made use of this chance. It waited on until the birds were flushed, then stooped, bound one and cleared off quickly. The sportsman was too bewildered by the jingling bells of the low-flying falcon to shoot before it was far out of range. Now it was once more a completely wild falcon, enjoying its freedom. Many of its kin, now on the screenperch in the Old Posthouse quietly awaiting their turn to be slipped at the heron in the afternoon, were to follow.

Mollen's complete survey encourages an attempt to express the performances of falcons and falconers in figures. The number of days in the period of May 4–July 12 excluding Sundays, public holidays and days with unfavourable weather, can be fixed at 48. This amounts to 1. 7 herons per day. In approximately the same period, Bots' team caught 74 herons, so it can be concluded that at least 3 herons were brought down daily. Unfortunately, it is not known how many falcons participated daily. To bring down 3 herons, at least 3 teams of 2 falcons each were needed, totalling 6 falcons. This number is in accordance with 6 seats on the cadge. It is known that at least 3 cadges were carried, so the number of flights not crowned with success must have been very large—beautiful and enthralling though they may have been. The survey of herons caught appears as follows:

Year	Falcons	Herons
1839	18	104
1840	22	128
1841	44	287
1842	44	148
1843	40	200
1844	36	100
1849	14	128
1850	16	138
1851	18	130
1852	36	297
Total	**288**	**1,660**

If we take for granted that in the years 1845–48, missing in the survey reports, the results were the same, then it may be concluded that in the years 1839–52 approximately 2,300 herons were caught. Not included in this number are the seasons 1853–55. Likewise, the herons brought down by the not yet fully trained novices between the beginning of April and the second half of May during all these years are not included.

The survey teaches us nothing about the individual performances of the falcons as they were flying in couples. If one takes this into account, the picture is as follows:

Year	Couples	Herons	Medium P. Couple
1839	9	104	11. 6
1840	11	128	11. 6
1841	22	207	13. 0
1842	22	148	6. 7
1843	20	200	10. 0
1844	18	100	5. 6
1849	7	128	18. 3
1850	8	138	17. 3
1851	9	130	14. 4
1852	18	297	16. 5
Total	**144**	**1,660**	**11. 5**

From these figures we can deduce that 144 couples caught (at least) 1,660 herons, an average of 11. 5 per couple. If we assume that the number of succesful and unsuccesful flights are in the proportion of approximately 1:1, this means that in a season of 48 days the falcons flew 23 times, i.e., every 2 or 3 days.

If one separates the years in which 7 to 11 couples were active from those wherein 18 to 22 couples were flown, it appears that in the first case the couples averaged 14. 5 herons and in the second 10. 4. In spite of 18 couples scoring 16. 5 in 1852, there can be no doubt that a smaller number of birds enjoyed more attention and better care, leading to better performance. As soon as falconers had to care for more than four birds, sufficient time and attention were lacking and performance decreased.

The falconer was more at home with his falcon's flight feathers than with the bookworm's goosequill. For this reason, properly printed forms were issued to the falconers to keep an accurate diary. No doubt they were willing to do so but had little time. It was at least between ten and half past ten at night before they were back at The Loo with horses and falcons that had to be cared for. If they had to look for a lost hawk it was often later than that. At the end of a laborious day they at last had time for a meal.

Van den Boom, for instance, had to be at Lake Uddel at sunrise to search for a lost falcon that like a fury, though in vain, pursued crows. Possibly the bird had pushed on to the lake hoping to kill a duck. The falconer still had a long ride that morning. Who in such circumstances is likely to keep the records painstakingly? The falconers indeed laboured from sunrise to sunset.

In 1849 new regulations were proposed that will not have pleased them:

> Art. 6 – Each chief-falconer is henceforth obliged to record in writing the outcome of the day: the names of the falcons, the quality of the flight, the location of the proceedings and the number of herons caught. This record has to be kept daily so that members of the Committee may control it at any time.

The Committee, appointed in 1840, was according to regulations composed of two Dutch and two English members and probably showed understanding for neglect of this rule. Anemaet, undersecretary to the late Prince Alexander and from 1848 secretary of the Club, a friend of both the chief falconers Bots and Mollen, would certainly have turned a blind eye to their problems. Besides, lack of records is no proof of inactivity. Be that as it may, much knowledge has been lost.

We are not informed about the percentage of falcons that got lost and the percentage of herons that were killed. We must assume that the former was high and the latter low. According to accounts of July 6, 1846, from both Bots and Mollen, they kept four and eight falcons respectively in the mews at Dfl. 6 each. At the latest, these hawks were born in 1845. In that year the falconers came to The Loo with, let us say, twenty-nine birds. Twelve of them were found worthy to be kept in service and so were settled in the moulting lofts at Valkenswaard. Possibly Newcome took one back to England. Maybe one was lost by being stabbed to death by a heron as happened to the falcon Prince of Orange after, together with Newcome's *Bulldog*, bringing down the last heron of the 1843 season. This was, however, a very rare occurence. Though improbable, a hawk could fail and end up prosaically in the workshop of the taxidermist or skin collector. Thus, starting from the twenty-nine birds at the beginning of the season, approximately half of them were lost. We assume that this number is on the low side.

As regards the herons, not many had to pay with their lives in the tournament: "The flight on the heron is the most beautiful of all, the more so because it rarely occurs that the falcons maul it so badly that it cannot be given its freedom." [92]

Unfortunately, we know little about the individual falcons and their careers. The story goes that three stoops were sufficient for *Bulldog* to bind his heron and bring it down. This falcon, netted in Valkenswaard in 1843, gained great fame because it was able to fly the heron without a teammate. This extraordinary bird came into possession of Newcome who said he had never had a better one. *Sultan* and *De Ruyter* too gained fame because they formed an extremely good team; in 1843 they brought down fifty-four herons and in the following year fifty-seven. These falcons also came into Newcome's service. We already mentioned the spectacular flights of *Napoleon*. Later, this falcon was again spoken of.

If the falcons had to deal with an adroit heron,[93] then the two veterans, *Napoleon* and *Nelson*, who never missed, were slipped. Whether it was an ironic freak of fate or a practical joke, we shall probably never know, but *Napoleon's* name was first coupled to his Prussian opponent, *Blücher*, and subsequently to his British opponent *Nelson*. So under the aegis of the Royal Loo Hawking Club the mortal enemies of Waterloo and Trafalgar at last came to cooperation.

It occurred regularly that herons, carrying one or more bands of previous years, were caught. It is again the famous Newcome who in 1843 caught a heron at Diddlington which had been banded five years before by Wilson's falconers. In 1844 it was banded a third time. Though it was not specifically done for scientific purposes, one could say that banding research was already being done at this time. It is also said that a heron, banded at The Loo, was recovered in Algeria.

The feats of arms described above can almost exclusively be attributed to the peregrine falcon, performer of the Haut Vol par excellence. What part did the gyrfalcons play? As mentioned before, transport from their far northern haunts to our regions cannot have done them any good. Moreover in our warmer climate they were far more prone to infectious and parasitic diseases than peregrines. Particularly frounce, a deadly infection of the throat, claimed many victims. But even the birds that survived travel and disease rarely made good as hunters. Their technique of flying low, in contrast to the peregrine, did not lend itself to the Haut Vol. They would not fly in couples without crabbing and quarreling. If the falconers succeeded in getting them to attack herons, this usually proved fatal to the heron and that was not the aim of the flight. In the same way, peregrines that developed the bad habit of breaking wings were put out of service. The gyrfalcon was not a succes. The falconers also had little or no faith in these specifically big falcons as is clearly shown in letters from Bots and Mollen. Bots' letter of February 3, 1846, here reproduced in full, reads:

> Your Honour will be informed that I received 4 Iceland falcons from Mollen 8 or 9 days after his return from England: no. 1 an old tiercel, two years in Mollen's care and good for nothing, another young tiercel and 2 young falcons, one of them ill when I received it. I informed Mollen of this next day and told him that it could not last long and it died a month ago. It could not swallow anything for 2 days before its death. The others are healthy and very tame, their primaries and tailfeathers we imped with needles as well as we could, but they cannot fly as they should. I am doing my best to train them properly. They are well on their way but nothing can be said as yet.
>
> I have 14 young falcons all of them adjusting very well and my 3 old ones are very beautiful and all moulted fine blue plumes. I have gutted the dead Icelander and preserved its skin. Please let me know what should be done with it. Now I address a kind petition to You and that is if You will do me the favour to send me money. I have to send my family 500 guilders within three weeks and besides we need much money in these expensive times. My friend Mollen is also in distress. Thank God all of us, except old Van den Heuvel who has a severe cold, are in good health including both our horses and those of Mollen.

It is clear that Bots had problems both with the gyrfalcons and other more prosaic matters. There is no doubt that the gyrfalcons about which he speaks belonged to the eight Mollen had collected from the Duke of Leeds on behalf of the Club. This gentleman indeed, as we learned earlier, sent his falconer Pells to Iceland in 1845, whence he returned with fifteen falcons. We may assume that Mollen and Bots each took four falcons into their care. Mollen, too, was no lover of gyrfalcons, as his letter of March, 1850, addressed to Anemaet shows:

> You ask me when we shall depart for The Loo; we intend to leave at the beginning of April for then we are in plenty of time. Because of the long winter with frost and snow, we could not proceed too well with the falcons. However they are developing reasonable, though up till now I have no expectations of the Norwegian falcons.

Only two gyrfalcons are known to have been succesful. In the beginning of the forties, probably in the seasons 1842 and 1843, the gyrfalcon *Zoë* distinguished itself[94]. This falcon scored eighteen herons. The other, called

Trophy from the Remembrance Stake Loo Meeting, 1849. Wood engraving by Joseph Sanders.
Private Collection.

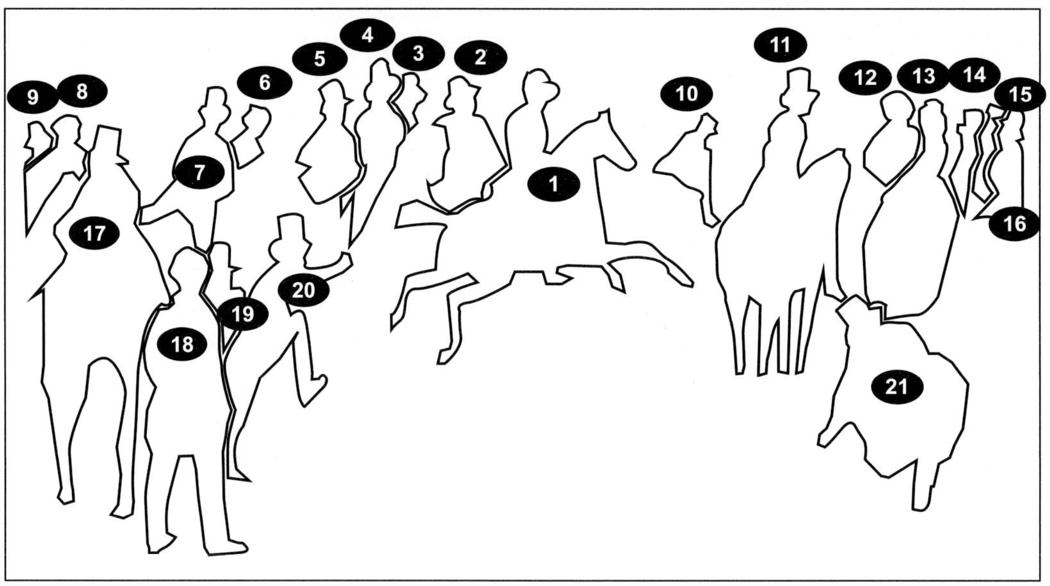

A group of falconers on the Soerense heath, in the middle, Prince Alexander.
Litho to Johann Sonderland.
Royal Collection.

1 Prince Alexander
2 Baron Sloet van Oldruitenborg
3 Baron Steengracht
4 Duke of Leeds
5 J. Winn Knight
6 Baron van Zuylen van Nievelt van de Schaffelaar
7 Baron Suffield
8 J. Gudin
9 J. B. Sonderland
10 Marquess Emmanuel d' Azeglio
11 Baron van Verschuer
12 H.C. Dubois
13 Baroness van Verschuer
14 Prof. Schlegel
15 P. Dubourcq
16 A. Verster van Wulverhorst
17 Van den Heuvel, falconer
18 P. Mollen, falconer
19 Arnold Bots, falconer
20 A. Mollen, falconer
21 P. Bekker, falconer

Morock or *Marock*, was netted by John Pells in Iceland in 1854. *Marock* was one of the eight falcons Mollen collected on behalf of the Club. Like some of the other birds, this gyrfalcon, came into Newcome's possession and then, unfortunately, got lost. It only enjoyed its liberty for a short time, returning to the well-known fields at The Loo, and before long caught by falconers who were training their hawks. All in all it was clear that the majestic hunter from

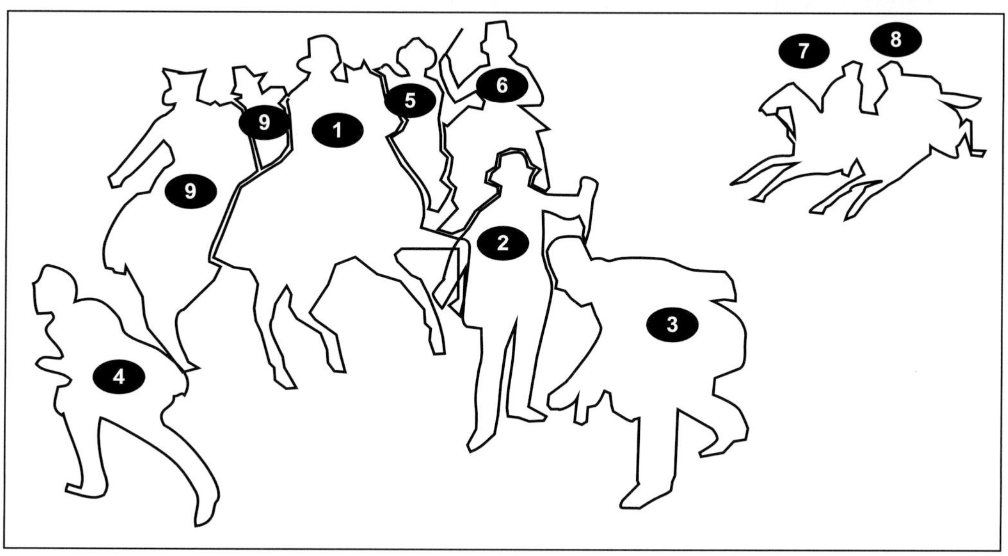

Falconers on the Soerense heath, in the middle, crownprince Willem. Litho to Johann Sonderland.
Royal Collection.

1 Crownprince William
2 E. Clough Newcome
3 J Bots, falconer
4 J. van den Boom, falconer
5 Sir A. Mallet
6 Baron von der Gablentz
7 Baron van Westreenen
8 Lord Millbank
9 Baron van Tuyll van Serooskerken
10 Duke of Leeds

the lonely and barren north did not thrive well in our regions. Even in the hands of the most experienced and able falconers it was of no use in falconry.

In the draft regulations of 1840 one can read: "The falconry season shall commence yearly on May 15th and end around July 10th. " In certain respects this was not valid for the falconers who, according to Article 8 of the regulations of 1840, were bound "to leave for the Loo with their assistants on April 1st each year. "

This meant that they had to be present six weeks before the club members arrived, but for what reason? The answer is clear. After St. Bamisday on October 1, the huts in the surroundings of Valkenswaard were occupied and the catch, which lasted for two months, could start. Training took five to six months so that birds caught in October could in the following March or April have reached the point where the last part of the training, namely flying the heron, could start. Where could this last phase of training better take place than around the big heronry at The Loo, where a large flock of herons was always present. Here they were first trained on low flying herons and later on the high flying ones. So by approximately May 15 the first-caught novices could be ready for real Haut Vol. It is now understandable that Prince Alexander, in his letter of June 19, 1840, expressed his pleasure in attending the training of the young hawks.

In the period in which they were caught, the young hawks were starting to mark out their own territory for hunting and spending the winter. For some of them it never came to that. They were netted and trained and since the finishing touch of their training—hunting—took place at The Loo, it became their hunting territory. This meant that they were less likely to flee their home territory and would sometimes return, thereby lessening the chance of being lost.

"Gentlemen I have the honour to announce the second round: three roasted herons." Drawing by Pierre Dubourcq.

À la Volte

It was in fact impossible to follow the Haut Vol without being a good horseman. As soon as the aerial combat became tense, it was important to be the first to reach the falcons on their heron because the aigrette was allotted to the first rider on the scene. It was a race without a defined course or finishing point.

Apart from this, regular races were also held. Both Crown Prince William and Prince Alexander were enthusiastic horsemen and so did much to promote the sport. And it goes without saying that the Club heartily joined in. On the Soeren Heath a racetrack and grandstand were erected for the Hawking Club Stakes. On June 27, 1844, Prince Alexander wrote to the King: "Tomorrow the stakes will take place in the vicinity of Soeren where an excellent field is at our disposal. There will be eight races; everybody is clad in costume. If the weather is favourable I think it will be a very entertaining day." The Prince himself had participated in the stakes on June 21.

A week after the famous stakes at Ascot in 1848 the stakes at Soeren took place. The program was as follows:

- The Hawking Club Stakes (for horses the property of members of the Hawking Club, to be ridden by them or their friends).
- The great Loo Stakes (for horses of all ages and countries, three years old).
- Steeple-chase and sweepstakes (to be ridden by members or friends of members of the Hawking Club).

It is clear that equestrian sports were not forgotten. The falcons, the falconers and their horses will have enjoyed these days of leisure.

Title page of a series of 21 pencil drawings by Pierre Dubourcq, 1842 (page 87 to page 97).
Royal Collection.

Breakfast in The Emperors Crown. On the wall the Club's deuce Mon Espoir est en Pennes. One of the gentlenmen is poring over The Times.

Clubmembers reading The Globe *and* The Times *in front of the The Anchor Inn, opposite The Crown Hotel.*

Before departure. Some gentlemen play a sort of "jeu de boule." The jack is a falcon's feather.

Preparations before the flights. Falcons are removed from the perch-screens to the cadges. One falcon is fed because she will not be in service today.

The falconry party on the way to Soerense Heath. Cadges are carried before the procession.

A baiting place. See the tell-tale sign board. Today it is the well-known restaurant Echoput.

Waiting for the herons.

The first heron comes within sight.

Mounting falcons, taking position to stoop. At right, a freshly caught heron is hooded and will be kept in custody to complete the training of the falcons that were caught late in the autumn.

The falcons are in hot pursuit. Members of the party are following and making a fast run to be first at the spot where falcon and heron touch ground with the aigrette being the reward.

The heron is brought down. At left, the other falcon came down on the lure. The falconer who took her up hurries back to the party. At right, a falconer in a uniform from the times of the French King Louis XIII.

Falconer swinging the lure to bring the second falcon back and down.

The party is waiting for the wind slowing down. In strong wind the herons fly low and the flights are not interesting.

It is raining, the falconers try to keep their birds dry.

Between the flights horse races were spontaneously organised.

Children from hamlets in the vicinity were entertained. The winner would earn a coin.

End of the day's activities. The gentlemen and the ladies depart for the hotels to dress for dinner. The falconers are feeding their falcons before carrying them home.

The arrival.

Reception at the Palace before dinner.

Dinner—left Crown Prince William and his spouse Princess Sophie; to the right is Prince Alexander.

After dinner—the bottles soon will be empty.

X The Reporters

—Dedicated to Henk Slijper.

... that the study of natural science became the guiding force in his life

The names of Schlegel, Verster van Wulverhorst and Wolf are well-known in the literature of falconry: the first two as authors, the latter as illustrator of the *Traité de Fauconnerie*. Without this study, a thorough reconstruction of falconry in the middle of the eighteenth century, particularly as regards the technical aspects, would not have been possible. Their names are closely related to the Club and a short sketch of these important personalities is the very least we owe them. Moreover, their characters are interesting enough to be worthy of our attention.

Schlegel wrote a very amusing sketch about his friend Verster van Wulverhorst in 1854. In 1884, Schlegel's son, the sinologist J. Schlegel, wrote a biographic sketch about his father, based on the latter's annotations. And finally in 1885, Palmer wrote an extremely interesting and sympathetic biography on Wolf.

Hermann Schlegel[95]

As the eldest of eleven children, Schlegel was born on June 10, 1804. He originated from a German patrician family. His father, David Schlegel, owned and managed a big brass foundry that manufactured copper ornaments for horse harnesses. Father Schlegel was a stern but good-natured man. He was very erudite, with a particular interest in Kant's philosophy and French literature. Young Hermann was subjected to a Spartan education, with Prussia's Kind Frederick II as his example. He himself wrote: "The most lenient rules in my education were being present in the study, at the stroke of 5 o'clock in the morning all the year round, with all study to cease at 10 o'clock at night. Excellent rules which became habit and are maintained by me till today!"

Already as a child, Hermann was keenly interested in nature, especially in beetles and insects. One day, he accidentally found a buzzard's eyrie containing eggs. From then on, his inquisitive mind centred on ornithology. He kept birds in aviaries and studied them intensively. Birds of prey in particular enjoyed his interest. He even tried to train falcons. In his grandfather's service was a gamekeeper called Geuther and through him, young Schlegel developed a liking for hunting. Moreover, he came into contact with a glass-blower who, like himself, was obsessed by nature and who taught him quite a lot. It was due to this friend that the study of natural science became the guiding force in his life.

Already at the age of thirteen, he contacted the ornithologist Naumann and the clergyman Brehm, both investigators and scientists whose names were to gain immortality. Schlegel, young though he was, had gathered so much knowledge that he attracted the attention of these naturalists. From his study, Brehm had an unobstructed view of a shrub frequented by a bird whose identification, according to Hermann, was wrong. During divine service he managed to kill the bird with his small-bore rifle. Proudly, he sneaked into the church, where Brehm was preaching the mercy of nature from the pulpit—the attitude towards nature must be devout and loving. Immediately after the end of the sermon, Hermann showed him his booty, an Icterine warbler. Back in the vicarage, Brehm spoke the prophetic words: "Let me embrace you, you are a genuine naturalist." To the young ornithologist, this encouragement was of no mean order.

Not long after, he met a Mr. Förster, who encouraged him to start drawing. Soon, Schlegel's talents for drawing with pencil and brush proved to be above normal. It was a gift he could make very good use of and which he continued to develop throughout his lifetime.

In the meantime, his schooldays ended and father Schlegel was of the opinion that he should prepare seriously for a profession. Although he had encouraged his artistic ambitions and given him a free hand in his study of natural history, he considered these as hobbies which would not earn him a living. They were unsuitable to one of a patrician family. He should go to the academy! But the boy thought otherwise. Theology was too narrow-minded, law too subtle, philosophy endless, linguistics silly, mathematics unimaginative and dull, and medicine, finally, too obscure.

So he entered his father's factory but it did not suit him. When one day his father remarked: "Without me you cannot keep your head above water," he departed without even saying goodbye. He found jobs at museums at Dresden and Prague as a bird stuffer and naturalist. In Prague, he was in the employ of the famous Haeckel. At last, in 1824, he arrived in Vienna.

In the meantime, he had earned some fame and recognition, so that in 1825 the well-known Temminck proposed he join his staff at the Museum of Natural History at Leiden. Schlegel gladly accepted the offer. However, the necessary means to undertake the journey were not at his disposal. Worst of all, he was called up for military service. He was now in a difficult situation. Since his departure, he had had no contact with his father who, just as stubborn as his son, had in his turn never tried to re-establish contact. But only his father could provide him with the required funds. He owed his father a great deal and he had sufficiently proved that he could stand on his own feet. In a way as original as it was energetic, he decided to solve the problem. With the few farthings he had in his pocket, he travelled to Altenburg where, late at night, he arrived at his parental home. He called loudly in French that someone urgently had to see Mr. Schlegel. Finally, the door was opened and father and son embraced each other. Influential relations and the need to make his way abroad sufficed to get him discharged from His Majesty's Service. So he was able to travel to Leiden where he arrived on May 25, 1825. In the museum he became assistant to Prof. Temminck.

Life at Leiden University did not meet Schlegel's expectations. He found the whole concern musty and the scientific level disappointing. This, however, did not prevent his soon feeling at home. As was his habit, he immediately started studying the Dutch language. The results were excellent and he learned to write his new language impeccably. He came to maintain many contacts with foreign naturalists, the ornithologist Kaup from Darmstadt, for example, and they often called upon each other. His contacts with Lucien Bonaparte about natural sciences were excellent. Schlegel had become a man of the world.

On June 22, 1837, he married Cornelia Budding. She was the daughter of the vicar of the Kaag near Leiden, a small island community surrounded by marshes, lakes, waterways and blue-grass meadows, a true paradise for birds. One may wonder whether it was wildfowling or the study of birds that brought the couple together. A son and daughter blessed the marriage. The former was to gain fame as a sinologist.

In the meantime, he had added to his respectable list of friends the Inspector-General of Hunting, Abraham Verster van Wulvenhorst. We may assume that this was the official who in 1838 drew his attention to the plans for restoring falconry at The Loo. It was an idea that must have appealed to Schlegel. Where better could he enlarge his knowledge of birds of prey than in falconers' circles? Later, he gave evidence of his interest in the course of things in a letter of September 12, 1842, addressed to the King[96]: "I have the honour to inform Your Majesty that I gave instructions to our correspondent, regarding the transport of the falcons from Copenhagen to Holland, to have the captain who is taking along the falcons, take such measures as he thinks necessary. I also asked him to inform Your Royal Highness either directly, if I should be absent, or otherwise through me if the usual means of transportation are to be considered as risky. I ordered the falcons to be cared for in the best possible way. In the meantime, etc. etc."

The two friends soon conceived the idea of recording this grand and, at that time, already unique happening in a book of the same quality. As yet, no indication has been found that Prince Alexander or Crown Prince William commissioned this work. However, it was dedicated to the latter, who had in the meantime become King William III.

Schlegel was too modest to provide the illustrations himself. His colleague

Professor Hermann Schlegel, by Johann Heinrich Neuman (1819-98).
Museum Naturalis Leiden.

and friend Kaup recommended a young man called Wolf, a self-taught artist who could draw animals realistically and in their natural surroundings. When visiting Leiden, Kaup showed Schlegel young Wolf's sketchbook and this led to the invitation to draw an old and a young goshawk lifesize. When Schlegel later saw these drawings, his choice was definitely made. Wolf's drawings were better than his and he was to illustrate the *Traité de Fauconnerie*. After this, Schlegel begged his friend, the editor Arntz, to have Wolf come to Leiden.

Anyone who studies the taxonomy of birds of prey in the *Traité de Fauconnerie*, will be impressed by the immense knowledge and exactitude that Schlegel brought to his subject. His creativity, intelligence and diligence made this work an everlasting monument.

Gradually, Schlegel's position in the museum became more important and on June 16, 1868, he was appointed director. In view of the papers he published, 237 in all, his scientific ambitions were in no way affected by this. He worked to the end of his life. On January 17, 1884, diabetes, which could not at that time be treated, ended his rich and prolific life.

Abraham Verster van Wulverhorst[97]

This gentleman was born at Bois le Duc on September 3, 1796. In 1828, Verster acquired the Seignorial Rights of Wulverhorst, situated between Woerden and Utrecht, and appeared ever after under the name of Verster van Wulverhorst. As with so many things, we should be careful not to flatter ourselves with the thought that we are original. In the middle of the nineteenth century, Salvin and Brodrick were already fervent bird protectionists. Verster van Wulverhorst could claim to be the first environmentalist. The presence of man in nature was an annoyance to him and he regarded it as "pollution."

He was a passionate sportsman and lover of nature, both qualities which made him eminently suitable to become Chief Forester and Inspector of Hunting in the district province of Zuid-Holland in 1833. Schlegel erroneously called his friend General Chief Forester and Steward of the Hunt. This probably originated from his regular contacts with the hunting members of the Royal Family. It goes without saying that Schlegel and he became intimate friends. In 1853, he founded the *Paper for Lovers of Hunting and Fishing* which appeared annually. Unfortunately, not more than five editions were published.

It is difficult to ascertain Verster van Wulverhorst's share in the monumental work, *Traité de Fauconnerie*. His contributions in the above mentioned papers hardly dealt with falconry, covering other subjects. Just as the falconers Bots and Mollen advised the authors regarding falconry, so probably Verster van Wulverhorst, a well-known authority in this field, collaborated on dogs.

Schlegel wrote a satirical short story about his friend called "A Wolf in Sheep's Clothing." Once, when attending a meeting of seriously minded and grave-looking scientists, better at home in a musty study than in the field, he detected a gentleman, ostentatiously clad in a sportsman's outfit, his friend Abraham Verster. "You here, Mephistopheles among naturalists, wolf in sheep's clothing!' Schlegel regarded his presence at this meeting as that of a drunk in a teetotaller's club, trying to discover what they were planning. Soon, both friends left the dry taxonomic lectures for what they were and discussed the ailments of Juno, Verster's beloved hound. Not in the least interested in the discussions, they designed the "systematics of the species scientisticus" and soon came to the conclusion that for all this sterile display of learning there was but one panacea—wildfowling.

There is reason to believe that he compiled the historical notes in the *Traité de Fauconnerie*. Furthermore, as mentioned above, we must assume that the dealt with the observations regarding dogs.

His insights into these creatures, whose makeup contains more human qualities than any other animal, have been corroborated by the most modern research. He suggest that human social instincts and feelings have been imprinted on them through the ages.

JOSEPH WOLF[98]

Joseph Wolf was born on January 21, 1820, at Moerz on the Moselle. His father had only two needs—good seasons for his crops and good prices. He was a farmer and also mayor of a dreamy village on the river, not far from Koblenz. Unflagging labour on the farm was the family's only source of wel-

Joseph Wolf by Lance Calkin.

N. A. J. P. H. van Es (1847–1921).

fare. His mother cultivated a flower and herb garden and this was what interested little Joseph. Every spring, he intensely enjoyed the awakening of nature. His first tool was a pair of scissors with which he cut out silhouettes of birds and stuck them on the windows. Though there was a great difference between the patrician household in which Schlegel was educated and the simple farmyard where Wolf grew up, they were both completely preoccupied by their love for nature and its investigation. This was so strong that each chose to leave home for an uncertain future.

During the winter as well as during school holidays, Wolf was expected to take part in work on the farm. He, however, preferred tracking the prints of marten in the snow. He liked sowing and planting, but hated caring for the horses. Already at a very early age, he was crazy about hunting and firearms. At the age of fourteen, he was given his father's old gun, a single-barrel flintlock. In those days he felt proud to be able to protect the chickens from the swift raids of the goshawks. In a world rich in birds and mammals, Wolf soon learned the art of snaring. He caught a couple of pine martens and made delicate paintbrushes by fitting the hairs into the quills of crow or thrush. Thus, he portrayed a long-eared owl he had kept in captivity. Much later he was to remark that birds of prey are good sitters for an artist, owls even better, but songbirds bad and mice even worse. Birds of prey particularly interested him.

In order to draw, he did not shoot his "bird models" but caught them. He cut a wedge in the tail of kestrels and so could recognise them when circling the steeple of Münstermayfeld, where they lived in a colony.

More and more, he began to hate the farm. When he was sixteen years old, his father realised that he could better yield: Joseph should become a lithographer! He managed to get an apprenticeship of three years with the Beckers

Brothers at Koblenz. His talents were soon recognised and he was allowed a free hand.

Apart from his work, he spent time studying birds in the surroundings of the town. He was also interested in literature. His biographer Palmer tells us that he was deeply impressed by a translation of Shakespeare. After his apprenticeship, it was difficult to get a job, though he had already set his sight beyond lithography. There was nothing for it except to return to the farm.

Besides working on the farm, he designed wine labels. He also went out shooting, considering his gun as a means of gathering knowledge. In the meantime, his abilities were discovered by Dr. Kaup, ornithologist at Darmstadt, who commissioned him to illustrate a study concerning Abyssinian birds. This led to an appointment at the museum where he illustrated and stuffed birds in his own original way. Being a qualified lithographer, he could earn some money from it.

When his patron Kaup, having attended a conference in London, visited Schlegel in Leiden, he took Wolf's sketchbook with miniatures with him. Schlegel was impressed and ordered Wolf to draw a young and an old goshawk in natural size. In the end, it was this order which led Schlegel and Verster van Wulverhorst to illustrate the *Traité de Fauconnerie*. Wolf got permission of absence to work in Leiden where he stayed with the editor Arntz. Schlegel asked Wolf to study waders and other birds, unfamiliar to him, in his spare time. To Schlegel's astonishment, his companion did not take his sketchbook along. Wolf, however, studied the birds with close attention and Schlegel was very impressed when he saw the pictures Wolf had drawn the evening after the excursion.

After a month, Wolf had to return to Darmstadt, having obligations there and, much though he regretted it, unable to stay longer. He was now a qualified lithographer but, as lithography "destroyed mind, breast and eyes," he foreswore this craft for once and for all. He had to fit himself for another means of earning a living and that required money. As he lacked the necessary means, he called upon his father, however without result. Luckily, he had friends willing to help him. So, although return to Leiden was not feasible, he said it was possible to draw the birds' portraits piece by piece and send them. This proposal was accepted. After finishing a picture, he put it aside for a week and then decided whether corrections were necessary. So his dispatches were delayed for a week and in a letter[99], dated August 14, 1843, he circumstantially apologised for this delay. When Verster van Wulverhorst nevertheless bade him come back to Leiden, he replied (September 15, 1843) that return was out of the question.

Illustrating gyrfalcons required some information (August 29, 1843): "Could their stature and movement be deduced from peregrine and merlin?"

Titlepage of the Traité de Fauconnerie with old and contemporary images. The size of the book is 76 x 59 cm.

In that case it would be sufficient to send him some more stuffed skins and precise and accurate descriptions of the unfeathered parts and their colour. When the pictures of merlin and sparrowhawk were discussed, he pointed out that it would be cheaper to combine these small birds on one page (October 20, 1843). In that case, however, minute detailing of the feathers would have to be abandoned. In this letter he also politely requested the remittance of 8 Louis d'Or, being the price of four paintings already delivered. Part of the remainder of the illustrations, accompanied by letters, followed up to and including December 1st of the same year. It was to take ten more years before the authors could present a copy, bound in red Moroccon leather, to King William III.

Wolf's reputation was made after his Leiden period. He overcame his financial problems and could look at his future with confidence. He obtained sufficient orders and was able to do well. Yet he was not content. Having saved some money, he enrolled in the Academy of Arts in order to improve his oil painting technique. It was during this period that Chief Forester Bauer introduced him to field sports. Bauer enjoyed Wolf's shooting abilities and he appreciated the perfectly natural way in which he portrayed birds according to his observations in the field while hunting. Wolf fruitfully combined shooting with the use of his sketchbook, in which he precisely recorded all the dimensions of the game, e.g., feet and toes. So, he combined hunting with art and science. Critical, correctly he remarked: "Studying animals, even in zoos, is more illustrative than looking at them along the barrel of a gun."

It was in this period that he concentrated on the study of backgrounds: "The animal portrait only appears to full advantage against the background of its natural surroundings. The picture becomes caricatural when the background is born of fantasy." What he meant, becomes clear in some of the pictures in the *Traité de Fauconnerie*, where the background was drawn, not by himself but by a lithographer. Wild falcons and eagles belong to the immense space of the sky and large canvasses. Indeed, a peregrine standing on the branch of an oak, surrounded by foliage, is just as unnatural as a goshawk on a tree stump.

By 1847, Wolf had seen enough of Darmstadt and in order to perfect his professional skills, entered Antwerp's Society of Art. His heart, however, was not in landscape painting. Again, Kaup helped him. Just back from an ornithological congress in London, he gave him a commission from the famous ornithologist, Gould. It was well known that Wolf had painted birds of prey beautifully for Schlegel and he felt honoured by this commission. Not long after, he was invited to come to England to illustrate Gray's *Genera of Birds*. So he started to work for Gray, who highly valued his technique—birds copied from real life and not as bird stuffers thought fit. Thanks to his endless observations in nature, he was able, using stuffed birds, to draw them as living beings.

It was not long before Wolf got to know one of England's most renowned painters, Sir Edwin Landseer. This gentleman said of him: "He must have been a bird before he became a painter." His friendship with Landseer was valuable to him. Wolf was introduced to the English landed gentry and became friendly with many. He also learned to know John Gould, former under gardener of the Royal Gardens at Windsor, very well. Interested in birds and stuffing them, he had worked himself up as an ornithologist of stature. Gould's rough character however, strongly differed from Wolf's. When he had got to know him better, Wolf said of him: "A sly old fellow, but the biggest lout I ever met." Nevertheless, bound by their common interests, both travelled in 1856 to Hjerkin (Dovrefjell) where, as Wolf later said, it was rather primitive. From there, they made a trip to Snae Haetten (Snöhetta) to watch birds. Back in London, Wolf began to work out his sketches. The woodcock, however, posed problems. He pictured this bird, sitting on its nest, because he did not know its posture when standing and walking.

Livingstone was another who made an appeal to his skills. Wolf, however, did not entertain his proposals because Livingstone understood nothing of animals. It was a sign that he had earned a position which allowed him to make such a refusal.

In the same year, Wolf exhibited one of his finest paintings at the Royal Academy[100]—two lightly coloured gyrfalcons on a kite they had bound. On behalf of Schlegel and Verster van Wulverhorst's work he had studied gyrfalcons and had, no doubt, seen them at Dovrefjell. Wolf, according to his style and technique, had paid close attention to the minutest details of this oil painting. A beautiful clouded sky in the background provided the space where these falcons belong. The work remained unsold and so, after the exhibition closed, he sold it to a gentleman farmer. This gentleman later sold it in his turn to Lord Lilford for the price of probably £600. When Lilford's collection was put up for auction, the painting changed into the hands of Mr. Scott, a devotee of falconry (BFC). The price of £9 was so low because other bidders had only made bids for the frame.

Nevertheless, his great ability for painting falcons posed problems to Wolf. According to him, their colours lacked the warmth of those of eagles and buzzards. He found it difficult to paint the oblique bandage of the falcons against the light background without using great contrast. When painting predators in action, it usually did not come off. He loved the goshawk that sees its prey disappear and is left with a bunch of feathers in its claws, or the fox contenting itself with the long tail of a pheasant.

In this period, Wolf enjoyed the height of his career. He was honoured to a high degree by men like Thorburn, Landseer, Gould, Schlegel, Salvin, Whymper and others. Even Charles Darwin valued him highly. He moved several times in London, the last time to Bernersstreet in 1860. Here, his excellent biographer Palmer often called upon him. In 1899, the rich and creative life of Joseph Wolf came to an end.

XI Downfall and End of the Club

The die is cast...

The Haut Vol was doomed. It was not lack of falcons or falconers that heralded the end, but other factors which played a part. Growth of the population, land settlement and industrialisation were cutting up the landscape, which would now bear the stamp of human activities forever. The horizon narrowed and the abundance of space, essential to the Haut Vol, and the splendour of the scenery with its inviolated and faraway horizon was lost. In England, these developments had already finished the flight at heron and kite, and it could be anticipated that events in Holland would turn out no different. Farmers and foresters had set greedy eyes upon the remaining wastelands. In 1847, the collectivised farmers (Order Mark) put up the heath along the way to Soeren for auction. The soil was poor and, although the process was slow, dependent as one was on horsepower and manual labour, cultivation in the nineteenth century could not be brought to a halt. The heronry was disturbed and in 1849 some birds moved and founded a heronry at the castle Biljoen, near Velp[101]. The fate of the Falconers' Club at Didlington was to be repeated. The end of the Haut Vol was inevitable, even at its last resource, The Loo.

In their initial enthusiasm, the members of the Club had misjudged other facts. Travelling in those days was uncomfortable and time consuming. English members had already in the thirties the advantage of a regular steamer-service to London[102], but we do not know how much time Prince Trautmannsdorf needed to come from Vienna; it took Adriaan Mollen, taking along falcons, nearly a month. For d'Offémont, the voyage from Compiègne, including ferries over the great rivers, at least two days were needed. It is quite understandable that the yearly return to The Loo imposed a rather heavy burden on some of the members. It goes without saying that attending the Haut Vol was not a matter of a few days. The accommodation of the hotels in these days could hardly compete with the luxurious mansions and palaces of the greater number of members.

It is well-known that costs were high. There was no refrigerator[103] available to preserve the costly beef for the falcons. Great numbers of pigeons were used, totalling from 1,200 to 1,500 at a price of Dfl. 0. 40 each. Maintenance of the horses was costly; throughout the year, the chief falconers Bots and Mollen, each had to look after two horses. It was not for nothing that the salaries of the falconers were attuned to the expenses they had to make. The

A group of falconers by Charles Rochussen (1814-94), watercolour dated 1856. A year before this the club was disbanded. This is a study to an oilpainting.
Valkerij en Sigarenmakerij Museum Valkenswaard.

level of these salaries ranged from two to four times as high as that of the average artisan[104]. Costs of lodgings and of entertaining guests at dinner parties were also high. And, finally, the cost of stabling one's own or hired horses and their maintenance appeared on the bill.

The Society boasted a large number of members. How many were true falconers and how many were sincerely interested in falconry? The number of falconers could almost be counted on the fingers of one hand. Newcome, for example, was one of the best. The second category was larger but not much. Those who joined after the first hour probably enjoyed earning the aigrette, but just how many of them really carried the falcon on fist is still an unanswered question. Members were attracted by the Society and its events, of which the Haut Vol was the most important. The participation of members of the Royal Family was certainly no less fascinating. Ultimately, there were too few real adepts of falconry to carry the burden of the Club.

The membership roll was anything but constant. Already in the forties, this became evident. In the autumn of 1847, Prince Alexander, being in poor health, set out for Madeira and his energy and enthusiasm were sorely missed. The enthusiasm of only a few propelled the Club to its lone and lofty height and this is little short of a miracle. But even for them, maintaining this level was in the end an impossible task. The tragedy of the end was manifested in the way the members passively allowed the Club's doom to be sealed. An entirely different reason[105] for the decline was noted by the Duke of Leeds—the King insisted on commencing dinner not later than ten o'clock in the evening. Consequently, the members had to leave the field at half past eight at the latest to be in attendance in due time, having refreshed themselves and dressed. Of course, the real lovers of the sport deeply regretted breaking off the game at its height. They had come far for falconry, not for dinner. Added to this, the unpredictable temper of the King did not always make attendance at dinner a pleasant affair, as has been mentioned before. Queen Sophie wrote to her intimate friend Lady Mallet[106] that, for this reason, guests often went home earlier. It is very well possible that these facts constitute an important reason why the Club lost its viability.

The death of Prince Alexander in February, 1848, removed one of the most important buttresses of the Club. His personality, more than his brother's, was very attractive to the members and his love of falconry had infected others with his enthusiasm. The already fading interest in the Haut Vol at The Loo was perceptibly decreasing. It manifested itself in less frequent participation of members and, even worse, in their paying their subscriptions late or not at all. Already on April 3, 1841, Tindal[107] advised Prince Alexander to interest and enlist more gentlemen in the province on behalf of the Club: "an extended membership would be agreeable to the Club and profitable for the accounts." From 1845 onwards, there were deficits.

The falconers also ran into trouble. They had their standing obligations and were in their turn dependent on paid contributions, which trickled in slowly, if at all. The treasurer even obtained printed reminder forms to send to the members. Initially, these forms stood in the name of Prince Alexander as President; after his death they were hand written in the name of King William III, for example:

> His Majesty the King of the Netherlands and Patron of the Royal Dutch Falconers' Society, ordered me in accordance with Art. 7 of the Regulations, to request you, being a member of aforementioned Society, to remit to me your contribution for 1849 for the amount of 100 guilders.

The first mention of difficulties by a falconer is, to our knowledge, a letter from Mollen, dated September 21, 1849, and doubtless also written in Bots name, addressed to Prince Alexander:

> I hope Your Highness will not take offence at my boldness in asking Your Highness to send us some money because we are in great need. It would be more economical if we could buy enough forage for the horses to keep a stock. In addition, the catching season is now at hand and this necessitates our paying many expenses which does not suit us at all, since we are hard up for money. We had hoped that Mr. Newcome would send

us some money on account, but as yet we have not received anything from His Lordship.

With all respect, etc. etc.

This letter puts it quite plainly. The falconers did not occupy all the huts themselves for the catch and needed paid helpers. So, the large advance expenses needed at the beginning of the catching season are easily explained.

The following year was no better. Prince Alexander was already ill and his departure for Madeira imminent. Mollen then addressed himself to his undersecretary, Anemaet, who in 1843 took over the treasury from Baron Sirtema van Grovestins. Anemaet was friendly with the falconers as is apparent from the beginning of his letter, dated September 23, 1847:

My dear Sir and Friend,

I have received your letter with the enclosed remittance for which I send you the receipt. We kindly request you to ask Prince Alexander to send us more as soon as possible. You may agree that Dfl. 150 is but a small quantity. There remains, however, a sum of approximately Dfl. 2000 which is daily increased by our expenses. We have already caught 9 young falcons, so the catch proceeds reasonably well. We are very pleased to hear that Prince Alexander is recovering and pray for the speedy return of His Highness's health.

Yours, etc. etc.

In 1848, after the death of Prince Alexander, Mollen's request came earlier as he had reason to expect more difficulties and he did not want to run any risks. Shortly after the season, on August 18, he thanked Anemaet: "So we feel very obliged for the money our provider procured for us." Nevertheless, the situation came to a head. In a letter dated March 12, 1849, Mollen, writing as spokesman of the company of falconers, stressed his urgent request for payment as follows:

I received your letter dated April 5th, enclosing money for which we sent you the receipt. Under the stress of bad times, we feel obliged to write to His Royal Highness, Prince Henry, to ask if His Royal Highness would be willing to send us more money. It is very disadvantageous and difficult for us to continue to advance money for expenses. Again, a big debt balance will remain at The Loo. I hope that next year matters will improve.

Yours, etc. etc.

Prince Henry was involved, because Crown Prince William had at that time bidden his country farewell and left for deer hunting in Scotland. The correspondence reveals that things were not going well. The falconers were badly paid and they worried about their future. The shortage amounted to Dfl. 1,900 in 1848 and again in 1849, Crown Prince William's year of inauguration. Owing to mismanagement, the inheritance of his father, King William II, was not yet settled and posed problems. Nevertheless, King

William III was generous with regard to falconry and loosed the strings of his private purse to meet the debts. He clearly demonstrated that his heart was in the Haut Vol and that he was anxious to maintain it. In 1850, the situation became even more trying and again he proved that he took it seriously. He now undertook to pay the expenses of one team, that of Mollen, entirely from his own account. The other falconers' expenses, however, remained the Club's responsibility.

In the same year, the regulations were finally settled. A commission of five members was appointed to enforce the rules and settle current affairs. The King was Patron and President and the duties of the Club's administration were, during the meeting of July 3, 1850, imposed on H. M. Baron Mollerus[108], a member since 1844. Furthermore, it was laid down that one member of the Commission of Control should supervise the falconers, assisted by the Duke of Leeds and Mr. Newcome.

Henry Marie baron Mollerus (1812-99), wearing the royal chamberlain attire. In the name of King Willem III he liquidated the Royal Loo Hawking Club.

When the season ended in June, 1855, it became clear that something had to be done. In an oral interview, Mollerus addressed himself to the Hon. K. W. de Kock, Director of the King's Cabinet and His Majesty's trusty friend. Mollerus asked him to inform the King about the financial situation of the Club. Accordingly, he then explained the situation in a letter to De Kock. From this it could be gathered that there were Dfl. 4,116. 20 in hand and that Dfl. 3,166. 68 had to be paid by July 1, leaving a balance of Dfl. 949. 52. At the same time, Mollerus pointed out that the year before, some members had asked him if he could continue the sport for another year by means of the money in hand and the incoming contributions. He mentioned that he had answered positively, providing the members would meet their obligations and pay their contributions. Furthermore, he wrote:

> In last January, however, I realised that continuation of the Club's expenses could not be met by the contribution of only 21 paying members[109]. So, through the secretary, Trossarello, I let falconer Mollen know that in July it would be decided whether or not the Club would keep on the falconers. I have, however, made no statement regarding the King's falconers but would recommend their future to His Majesty.

From this letter, it may be concluded that Mollerus saw no more possibilities. He requested His Majesty's permission to pay out Dfl. 3,166. 68 on July 1st and subsequently to be informed about next year's planning. Thus, Mollerus drew a clear distinction between the falconers of the King and those of the Club. Quite rightly, he placed the destiny of the former in the King's hands.

De Kock took counsel with the King and in a letter dated June 21, 1855, let Mollerus know:

> His Majesty believes that the Society "had better die out." You can take such measures as you think fitting for the conclusion of the matter and may dismiss the falconers. I forwarded your message to His Majesty who was sympathetic.

One could envisage more suave and elegant instructions from the King, as he was President of the Society. Their final execution was delayed, but not for long. Mollerus could not wait, because the treasury, his responsibility, was empty. In view of the feelings and opinions of the members, he realised all too well that it was senseless to convene a meeting. He drafted a circular for the Dutch members, dated July 1:

> Undersigned, commissioned at the meeting of July 3rd, 1850, to conduct the administration of the *Koninklijk Nederlandsch Valkeniers-Gezelschap*, begs to inform you that the said society counted 21 Dutch and, this year, 2 English paying members.
>
> Exceptional circumstances diminished the number of herons on the Royal Shoot at Apeldoorn to such an extent that the results of hunting will be unsatisfactory.
>
> The amount in cash is insufficient to maintain the hunting team properly.
>
> His Majesty, Patron of the Society, has been informed and has authorised the undersigned to propose to the members that the Club be dissolved. The funds to this end are available. The accounts may be inspected by persons concerned at the house of the undersigned during the month of January 1856.
>
> Finally, the undersigned having, up to and including August 1st, received no objections to above mentioned proposal from sufficient members to form a majority, will consider this as paramount to approval, whereby above named Society must be considered as having ceased to exist.
>
> Gravenhage, July 1st, 1855. H. M. Mollerus.

He sent it with a covering letter to the King, the Queen and the Princes Frederick and Henry, requesting that he be informed about eventual wishes. Both the remaining English members of the Commission, Leeds and Newcome, must have been informed beforehand, so there was no need to approach them by means of a circular. Reactions were expected within a month.

During this period De Kock was staying at The Loo. Mollen, too, was present, engaged in finishing the season 1855—the last one. They discussed the circular and, on July 4, 1855, De Kock wrote to Mollerus, doubting its correctness: "... though the affairs of falconers and falcons are completely strange to me."

Moreover, he asked whether the dismissal of the falconers concerned the King exclusively and whether he was justified in dismissing them without consent of the members. If not, it would be prudent to convoke the members for discussion of the matter and the possible continuation of the Club.

Finally, he remarked, "that Mollen had left Prince Trautmannsdorf on well defined terms, namely a lifelong appointment. This accords him rights which, though not covered by law, have nevertheless to be respected." In his deliberations with de Kock, Mollen had referred to Van den Heuvel's letter, dated July 18, 1840, in which Tindal in the names of d'Offémont, Newcome and

Stuart Wortley, asked him to come to The Loo where they guaranteed him "a good living for the rest of his life." It was understandable that Mollen was anxious about his future. He was forty-one and, highly specialised in the Haut Vol as he was, where would he be able to find employment? Though waiting on was practiced in England and Scotland and regarded as a valuable substitute and the flight at rooks was promising, he lacked the experience to compete with his English colleagues.

In a confidential letter in French, Mollerus replied to de Kock: "From your letter of July 4th, I gather that the falconer Mollen called upon you to protest. Please permit me to give you some information."

He let him know that he had sent out the circular and that he would justify himself in the meeting to come. He also mentioned his wish to resign from his administrative post. Next he wrote that he realised very well that the majority of members had refrained from cancelling their membership "so as not to be discourteous to the King." He also brought to the fore that he had already warned Mollen two years previously that the end was in sight and that the Society had refunded the expenses of falcons and horses. "Why should he bemoan his lot? The King's falconers are under His jurisdiction and they will have to apply to Him." Finally, he stated that he had informed the falconers of the Society about their approaching dismissal. He would pay them until January 1 of the next year. "After all, these gentlemen are not officials but merely servants." The expiration of the fixed term, August 1, 1855, had to be awaited. Mollerus' expectation was correct; on this fateful morning the post box remained empty. Without exception, the members maintained a stony silence and so executed sentence, earlier pronounced by the King. In the first week of September, Mollerus accordingly informed the Duke of Leeds and Mr. Newcome:

> Your Grace,
>
> I beg to inform Your Grace that His Majesty the King and the Dutch members of the Royal Loo Hawking Club have resolved to break up this Company. Consequently, I have the Honour to request Your Grace, being one of the Committee to make this resolution known to the English members; at the same time to intimate to Your Grace that the final accounts will be deposited for examination at my residence during the month of January next.
>
> I have the Honour to be Your Grace's obedient servant, A. H. Bn. Mollerus.
>
> To Edward C. Newcome His Grace Esq. the Duke of Leeds

Mollen, alarmed at the late arrival of the payments, addressed a petition to the King on July 20, in which he mentioned his entering His Majesty's service in 1840: "He had given up a very profitable position at Prince Trautmannsdorf, because he had been given to believe, and even promised, that he would be in service as falconer to the King for the rest of his life." His request was soon to be dealt with. A week later, on July 27, the Chief Steward of the Royal Hunt, E. L. Baron van Tuyll van Serooskerken van Vleuten, returned the request to the Director of the King's Council de Kock, observing that he could not advise, since the conditions of Mollen's appointment were not known to him. Mollerus could best clarify the situation.

Obviously, Mollerus advised in his favour, because a letter from the President of the King's Council, Count Dumonceau, dated August 28, recommended: "The Royal Commission respectfully takes the liberty of proposing that Your Majesty grant the applicant a pension of Dfl. 400 a year."

The King accepted the proposal and the Royal Commission authorised His Majesty's Treasurer to pay the applicant the recommended sum in three monthly terms, according to the King's decision, as from January 1, 1856. This document was dated August 29. Mollen was very content with his pension: "I hope to enjoy it for 40 years."[110] The prophesy nearly came true.

Among the correspondence of the liquidation is a letter from Mollerus, dated December 9 and addressed to Mollen:

> I write to you at the request of the King's Treasurer. I suspect that it concerns His Majesty's order regarding your pension. Matters have been settled entirely without my knowledge, so I have not been informed about the conditions. I received no answers to my last circular, addressed to the members of the Hawking Society, so the Society can be considered to be liquidated. Wherefore I give you to understand that the wages will be paid until ultimo December next, whereafter the falconers in service of said Society shall be dismissed. Will you please note that I shall be abroad until November 1st.

After the last wages had been paid in December, a small credit balance remained. On February 2, Mollerus wrote, requesting the King's assent to his proposal to spread payments of this remainder:

> The credit balance in cash amounts to Dfl. 745. 07½. I take the liberty to request Your Majesty's assent to distribute this amount among the personnel of the disbanded Society; namely to meet master falconer Mollen's expenses for forage during the last 2 years and furthermore the other hunters who, owing to the cessation of the Club, have been dismissed and are latterly in distressed circumstances. I therefore propose the following distribution:

A. Mollen	Dfl. 300	Peels	Dfl. 80
P. Bekkers	200	Hunters at The Loo	45. 07½
P. Mollen	100	Toll-collector	20
Van den Boom	100		

The King approved and in February, 1856, Mollen rendered thanks:

> In the name of all our company I express our thanks to our Honoured King for the payments. I am sincerely grateful for all the care taken on our behalf. Please accept our compliments including those of our respectful servant. etc. etc.

The receipt, signed and returned by Mollen, also showed the signatures of P. Bekkers and P. Mollen, falconers to the King. We also encounter the names of Peels and Van den Boom (Booms), both falconers in the service of the Club. It is possible that it was only through Mollen that Van den Boom received an allowance of Dfl. 100 and that this must have reduced Bekkers' share.

The story does not end here. Many years later, Mollerus, then living in Potsdam (Berlin), received a letter from the Dutch ambassador, Count Van Byland, dated December 23, 1867. He was requested in the King's name to return some documents and bills relating to the Society, if they were still in his possession. They had not been found elsewhere. On New Year's Eve, Mollerus replied that he had delivered the documents, then under his care, to the King's palace. He had kept only those documents that had discharged him and was willing to have copies of these made. Moreover, he remarked that after twelve years his memory might fail him. Later on, Mollerus fixed a short note in German to this copy: "Count Van Byland told me that Crown Prince William had the intention of re-establishing the Society, but that there were no funds available."

After the death of Princess Wilhelmina, the former Queen Wilhelmina, her secretary, Mr. Thijs Booy, mentioned in his sensitive book, *It is growing silent at The Loo*, published in 1963: "When she wanted to reintroduce falconry, being such an essential part of The Loo and practised by her father, King William III, she refrained because the costs were too high." In high age, she even regretted these estimates of revenue. Sometimes, the past is quite close to us!

How did those gentlemen fare who had been so closely related to the well and woe of the Club? First of all, the Patron, King William III. He is reported to have continued falconry after 1855. In the inner circle of friends (Van Es, 19) he practised the sport in 1856 at least with some falconers from Brabant and Limburg, possible witness being a watercolour painting by Rochussen, signed 1856. Certainly it did not last for long. Cultivation proceeded and more and more herons left the colony. At last, the King gave up and had his gamekeepers destroy the heronry to prevent irreparable damage to the forest.

Adriaan Mollen, as we know, fared very well. Frans van den Heuvel's letter promising a good future "for the rest of his life," was a godsend.

Of his brother Paul it can be said that his hands were good for nothing else but carrying a falcon and swinging the lure. He got his Dfl. 100, had Adriaan render thanks to the King in the proper way and was unemployed. Understandably, he made a pathetic appeal to the King:

> The suppliant was until today employed as falconer to the King. Owing to the disbanding of the Society, payments connected with his service terminated on January 1st.

A dark future awaits him as a term of service since 1840 has prevented him acquiring other means of subsistence.

He is hopeful that his loyal devotion to duty will induce His Majesty to take an interest in his fate. He therefore, with all reverence and in all modesty, wishes to appeal to Your Majesty, so that Your Majesty will be graciously pleased to provide him with some sort of employment. Thus, an old servant could prove his loyalty, etc. etc.

By asking for employment and not for a pension, Paul had different tactics.

However valid his arguments, the Court Commission advised negatively. As mentioned earlier, Paul was lucky and could in the end take up his old craft in England. Of course, many Englishmen who appreciated his abilities at The Loo, knew him very well. Also, both his brother Adriaan and Bots had connections there. Obviously, Paul was good friends with Bots. When he embarked on April 15, 1861, to enter Lord Lilford's service, Bots accompanied him "to help get him started."[111]

What of Peer Bekkers? We find this able falconer on Mollen's register of 1853. So he was one of the chosen few who were to serve their time up to and including the last season. In 1857, he acquired the position of attendant of the birds of prey in the service of the Society Artis Natura Magistra at Amsterdam[112]. He died on August 27, 1859, having served for only two years.

The falconer Johan Peels succeeded Bekkers in Amsterdam. He was the man who succeeded Adriaan Mollen in the service of Prince Trautmannsdorf and later, probably in 1849, was appointed falconer to Bots' team. In the critical year 1850, however, we find him on Mollen's register together with Van den Boom, Bekkers and Paul Mollen. On November 12, 1896, Peels died at the age of seventy-two.

Last, but certainly not least, how did Jan Bots, doyen of the falconers, fare? As mentioned earlier, the Royal Loo Hawking Club owed its existence to him, and he was the only one who had witnessed the ups and downs of the Club ever since. He had made dangerous trips to Norway to catch gyrfalcons for the Club. In 1839, he had accompanied Newcome and Van Tuyll van Serooskerken, but in 1841 he travelled alone[113] as falconer to Prince Alexander. When in 1849 the necessity to economise became imperative, Bots and Mollen were ordered to attend with no more than twelve falcons each. In the documents of 1850, the year in which the King employed one team on his own account, Bots' name is no longer found[114]. Mollen then had four instead of two men at his disposal: Bekkers, Van den Boom, Peels and his brother Paul.

It is to be assumed that these falconers were in service up to and including the last season in 1855. In the detailed discharge papers of Mollerus, recorded in letters and official documents, Bots' name never occurs. There can be no doubt that, had he played a role after 1850, he would have been mentioned like the other falconers. He felt that the granting of a pension to Mollen but not to himself was an injustice with which he could not come to terms. He sent petitions, but in vain. In the end, on October 17, 1862, he received a definitive and negative decree and died in 1864, an embittered man.

These facts lead us to the conclusion that Bots was dismissed after the season of 1849. Economies in the Club in 1850, as well as the fact that Bots belonged to the senior ranks, may have caused his dismissal. It also becomes evident that, according to the practice of those times, he was unable to claim any allowance of pension. So, in 1850, when William III took one team on his own account, the Society dismissed Bots, chief falconer of the other team. The falconers of the latter came under the command of Mollen. Thus, only one team remained. The score of captured herons, however, shows that this considerably cheaper organisation functioned very well.

Finally, we must state that the highlights of the Royal Loo Hawking Club were in the years 1839–48, the period in which the inspiring enthusiasm of Prince Alexander carried the Club to a "pitch of excellence never before achieved."[115] After his death, the activities declined until in 1855 the members ignored the Club both figuratively and literally.

Concluding Words

—In grateful remembrance of Otto Kals from Düsseldorf

In western Europe the end of the Haut Vol in 1855 was not the end of falconry. More and more amateurs, enraptured by the flight of the falcon, learned to command the art and gradually began to take the place of the professionals. Rook hawking and waiting on began to flourished. Passage falcons and well-hacked eyasses were at their disposal. This happy state of affairs was maintained up to and including the first decade of the twentieth century. After World War II the number of those who were, for some reason or other, interested in falconry, increased enormously and out of all proportion, and it was said that falconry was blooming. But was it?[116]

In this survey, falconry in the first half of the nineteenth century has been described. Roger Upton (1980, 1987), covering the second half of the century and the first decade of the twentieth, elucidated our insight in the sport and its votaries. Without claiming some completeness, it can be stated that sufficient facts and items are now available to make a comparison between the weal and woe of falconry of those past times with those of the present day.

It is remarkable that in those days, which offered plenty of opportunity for the practice of falconry (except the Haut Vol), there were but a few falconers. It is even more remarkable that their number agrees with that of today's falconers in the same order of magnitude.

In our time, however, the serious onslaught we have made on nature has diminished the possibilities for continuing the sport in a proper and responsible way. Nevertheless, both the number of clubs and their membership increase rapidly. Cade (1982) remarks about this phenomenon: "Unfortunately falconry attracts an unusual number of eccentrics, exhibitionists, and extremists of one variety or another to its ranks. The types almost never turn out to be skilled falconers, but they make a very bad scene—sometimes for years—in their attempts te be falconers; and what is even worse, they frequently abuse the birds that fall into their hands." The reason is obvious but belongs to the field of the psychologist and does not fit into the scope of this critical survey.

It is a well-known fact that rulers and monarchs allotted the greater longwings to themselves, allowing the shortwings to the lower social classes. It is generally assumed that the falcons were kept as status symbols. But were they? Were these noble birds indeed needed to strenghthen the status of the illustrious highnesses? Their castles, lavishly decorated with tapestries and paintings and their garments, richly beset with jewels, their private armies and vast estates, their privileges of hunting and falconry showed their wealth and power. Their exalted status was sufficiently secure and did not need to be strengthened. Falcons were a normal part of the royal household—no less, no more. Their masters had themselves portrayed in all their glory, often in full-regalia and well armed. They left us an inheritance of thousands and thousands of portraits, but how many were pictured with a falcon on fist? In comparison only extremely few. Moreover, the goshawk, with its piercing eyes and formidable talons, would have been a better symbol of power and authority. They, however, preferred the falcon with its far less martial appearance and lofty flight. The falcon catches, then kills and then starts pluming and feeding. The shortwing catches and starts feeding brutally where the talons got hold, and therefore the sport was named Falconry.[117] Status symbolism, defined as overcompensation of intrinsic shortcomings with extrinsic means to stress one's individuality and importance, can possibly have played a role, but at best it was a minor one.

Practicing falconry in the community of the Royal Loo Hawking Club was devoid of status symbolism and so remained after its dissolution. Among those who exerted themselves to continue the sport after 1855, Edward Clough Newcome, we must assume, was the most prominent. In this period amateur falconers gradually began to replace the professionals and the sport was carried on at the highest level, merely for the sake of its beauty and enthralling qualities. There was no question of a status symbol. It was the falcon in flight and stooping that counted rather than the man who carried it on his fist.

After World War I falconry once more came into the limelight, the number of clubs and clubmembers slowly increasing. In inverse proportion to the dwindling facilities, these numbers soared after World War II, hand in hand with status symbolism, its unwanted side-effects and despite frightening decline of birds of prey, hunting birds in particular. An ominous tryptich! So not only intrinsic factors sustained the sport but extrinsic ones entered the scene. To make a long story short: true falconers were overwhelmed in number by people who carried odd birds of prey on fist or kept them as pets, set low standards regarding flying and killing wild quarry, well able to evade attack, and gave themselves the proud title of "falconer." Needless to say, this deplorable development was harmful to real honest falconry and inevitably lowered its general image in public opinion. In its wake, the new generations set low standards.

Already in the 1870s Jack pointed to the fathomless and unbridgeable abyss that exists between wild falcons, cheetahs, etc., on the one side and dogs, horses, pigeons, poultry and other domesticated animals on the other.

The former moulded by nature according to the law of survival of the fittest (and best), the latter man-made and imprinted to meet man's own specific and unnatural requirements.

The art of falconry starts with manning and training the wild creature, retaining the natural qualities it gained in the hard school of nature. It should in the end only pay attention to the prey of the falconers' choice and not to the large variety of prey it used to command in freedom and which it still commands. It requires passionate love, experience and an equivalent of green fingers to bring success to this. The art of training the wild hawk is practically a thing of the past and should be considered as a bad loss.

The introduction of captive-bred birds made the challenge of this delicate and difficult part of the training superfluous. Training of those, compared to the passage falcon does not require much ability or exertion, even when breeding met the needs of keeping the eyas wild and untouched by man. Training and flying of these illiterate birds represents in fact no more than imprinting them on one and the specific prey.

Several expert falconers in the period after 1855 compared the merits of well-hacked eyasses with those of the passage falcons (pearls beyond price) and unanimously acknowleged the inferiority of the former. At present captive-bred birds, all to often imprinted with disagreeable habits and bad manners, are on an even lower rung of the ladder. Whether or not they can after many seasons of flying and killing, reach the status of the passage falcon is very doubtful. Who is at present qualified to compare and to judge? The use of captive-bred birds has undeniably lowered the high standards of falconry.

In a number of sports the cup is won on the drawing table of the scientist, rather than by the talents of the driver or skipper. The presumptuous endeavour to better something already ideal through hybridization places the result on the wrong side of the abyss. What has biotechnology, that is, genetic manipulation, to offer in future? Will we see a bird with a double pair of lungs thereby enabling it to mount higher? Or perhaps there will be a bird that can be steered by a sophisticated telemetric device? Are not creatures of great nobility degraded to the ranks of man-made fowl? An equal mixture of claret and water may quench the thirst but doesn't taste good.

The question arises whether flying captive-bred birds meets the requirements of the real falconer. There can be no doubt that Mollen and Bots would have wrung their necks or had them dispatched to the bird stuffer. There are still falconers today who consider them unworthy of the sport and take the consequences with bleeding hearts.

Falconry is an age-old human activity of high cultural value and it should be saved as such. At present the cards lie open, mainly thanks to "falconers"—it is flying captive-bred birds or not flying at all.

Maybe that the captive-bred falcon is justified if one is deeply convinced and conscious of the fact that, striving and hoping for better times, it represents no more than a serious attempt to conserve falconry as a deeply rooted human right.

End notes

Preface

1 Col. N. J. A. P. H van Es was born November 18, 1847, on the Frisian isle of Terschelling. He entered service at the Military Academy of Breda at the age of seventeen and, on March 1, 1868, was appointed captain to the distinguished and exclusive Corps Mounted Artillery. Prince Alexander was Hon. Commander to this small military outfit. Failing health forced Van Es to resign on November 15, 1898, with the rank of Major. He was an artist and a man of letters and in this capacity published in 1908 *The Historical Museum* in twelve folio volumes at his own cost. The last volume dealt with Prince Alexander and falconry at The Loo, in particular the Royal Loo Hawking Club. Hoynck van Papendrecht illustrated the work and the rich ornamentations and copies of drawing by Wolf, Sonderland, Dubourcq and Van Loon were all coloured by Van Es himself and Roskam. The intention was to present the costly series to retiring officers on condition that it be returned to the Corps on death, so as to keep it within the Corps. The number of retired and living officers may very well fit into the number of fifteen, presumably the number of the published series. It came to nothing and only very few intact copies, containing the part dealing with falconry at The Loo, could be traced. It is possible that personal information from the elder officers, who might have known Prince Alexander personally, enabled Van Es to complete his biography of the Prince with interesting items. Van Es died on February 8, 1921.

2 Prof. A. E. H. Swaen was born on February 9, 1863. Already at the of twelve he got his first lessons in English from Mrs. Swindels. At nineteen he became tutor to the children of the family Rivers, Sawbridgeworth, Herefordshire, where he learned to appreciate the life of the landed gentry and became interested in ornithology. In 1904, he became assistant-professor at the University of Groningen, commissioned to researching old English drama. At the same time, he was honoured with the honorary membership of the Royal Hungarian Ornithological Society. His appointment as Professor of English literature at the University of Amsterdam followed in 1913. Soon, he became a member of the board of the Dutch Society for the Protection of Birds. Owing to his merits concerning the history of falconry and to his manifold English connections (Blaine, Savory, "Harry the Hawker"), he earned the Honorary Membership of the British Falconers Club. Swaen was active in founding the Dutch club Nederlands Valkeniersverbond Adriaan Mollen. Shortly after the club's annual meeting at Amsterdam, he died on October 29, 1947, at the age of eighty.

Publications:

Mute to mute, mutings: muetir. Studia Neophilologica 3, 1918.

De Valk in de Iconographie, ed. Aerts, Maastricht, 1926.

Enige valkeniersuitdrukkingen bij Froissart en zijn Hollandschen Verteller. Studia Neophilologica 14, 1929.

Slechtvalk. Studia Neophilologica 15, 1930.

The Booke of Hawking after Prince Edwarde Kinge of Englande and its relation to the book of St. Albans. Studio Neophilologica 16, 1932.

De Valkerij in de Nederlanden, Thieme 1937, already mentioned.

De Cura Accipitrum, Adelard of Bath, Allard Pierson Stichting, 1937.

"Enkele mededelingen omtrent de Valkenjacht." Jaarverslag *Koninklijk Oudheidkundig Genootschap*, Amsterdam, 1952

Woordenlijst der Nederlandse Valkenierstaal (1937?).

3 Dr. J. M. P. van Oorschot was born on May 23, 1938, and he is today historian at Eindhoven. Valkenswaard is situated in the vicinity, where he teaches history and politics and so Van Oorschot, social sciences and history being his field of research, came upon the importance of falconry to this village. Through his studies he made contact with the families Mollen, Bots and Peels and also with G. A. van Nie and J. Van Gerven, both interested in the history of falconry and practising the sport. His investigations culminated in *Vorstelijke Vliegers en Valkenswaardse Valkeniers sedert de 17de Eeuw*. It earned him the title of Dr. Phil. He treated his subject exhaustively, providing us with a wealth of knowledge about Valkenswaard and its falconers in particular.

Besides other studies, he published:

Valkeniers zonder Aureool, 1974.

De Valk tussen Leeuwerik en Gallische Haan, 1975.

De Hoge Vlucht van de Valk in het Duitse Taalgebied, 1976.

These studies are published in the *Jaarboeken van het Nederlands Valkeniersverbond Adriaan Mollen.*

I Introduction to Falconry

4 Jesses: leather straps, fastened to the legs of the falcon with a special knot.

5 Halsband: adopted unaltered from the Dutch vernacular. Fine cord of braided silk around the neck of the bird, the loose end of which dangles between its legs. It has been said that falconers used the halsband to "strut" the bird when galloping. Not in use in western Europe. Depicted on Persian miniatures.

6 Gyrfalcon. The male is called jerkin. *Falco rusticolus*.

7 Shortwing: hunting bird, belonging to the *accipitridae*. E.g., goshawk and sparrowhawk have relatively short, rounded wings, contrary to the falcons (longwings) whose wings are long and pointed.

8 King of Sports: The saying is "Falconry King of Sports and Sport of Kings," exactly expressing the real falconer's feelings about his sport.

9 Haut Vol: French, lit. High Flight, used for the flight of heron and kite. See chapter 10, Van de Wall (2001).

10 Manning: acquainting the falcon to man.

II The Origin of the Club

11 Kite and black kite, respectively *Milvus milvus* and *Milvus migrans*.

12 Upton (1960).

13 It is said to have happened several times that the Club's falcons, when flown elsewhere and lost, returned to The Loo. Salvin & Brodrick, 1855. The author used the facsimile of 1971.

14 Sloet van Oldruitenborgh, Van Rechteren, Prince Alexander and Van den Heuvel wrongly wrote Stuard Worthley instead of Stuart Wortley.

15 Upton (1980).

16 Vincent Gildemeester Baron van Tuyll van Serooskerken, was born at Bath in 1812 and was related to the Walpole family. Like his niece, Alexandrine Tinne, he was an adventurous cosmopolitan. In 1844, he married Charlotte Mansfield in London. Like many of his family, he served the Dutch Court as chamberlain. In 1852, he founded the successful Billiton Tin Company. Van Tuyll and his wife were on intimate terms with Queen Sophie. On March 17, 1860, he died at The Hague.

16a One of these falcons is depicted in Salvin & Brodrick (1971). The Royal Loo Hawking Club.

III The Royal Loo Hawking Club

17 Baldick (1970).

18 Van Es (1908) mentions N. Tindal, it was in fact Henry Tindal.

19 Apart from forage, maintenance of horses and harnesses, travelling costs, etc., we find on this account:

8 falcons moulting in the mews at Dfl. 6	Dfl.	48
112 bands for herons		6. 82
Salary A. Mollen		800
P. Bekkers		300
P. Mollen		280

Mollen made a mitake in his calculations; the correct amount was Dfl.2812. 04, not Dfl. 2812. 54.

Concerning the year 1846, Bots' total account amounted to the considerable sum of Dfl. 2975. 22. Among many other items, chiefly expenditure for maintenance and hire of horses, we find on this account:

Falconry	Dfl. 40. 0
4 Falcons mounted	24. 0
Mr. P. Bakker for patrolling the heronry	1. 5

IV The Patronage of the House of Orange

20 See Bornewasser (1977), Bosscha (1852), Doorn (1977), Tamse (1977).

21 During the Napoleonic occupation of the Netherlands, King William I was exiled and left for England, not intending to return.

22 Dutch sovereigns are not crowned, but inaugurated.

23 In spare time horse stakes were organised on Soeren grounds.

24 Roedeer, not deer, existed in this region.

25 Van Es (1908), Royal Collection.

26 Lady Malet was married to the English ambassador at The Hague. In 1984, Hella Haasse and S. W. J. Jackman published the elaborate correspondence of Queen Sophie and her intimate friend Lady Mallet.

V The Falconers

27 In early times, Valkenswaard was called "Verckenswaard," owing to its pig-market (*vercken* means pig) which existed at the same time as the falconers' trade, Swaen (1937), Van Oorschot (1974).

28 Models of huts and catching devices can be seen in the Municipal Historic Museum at Valkenswaard and in the Museum of Game and Game-Management at Doorwerth, near Arnhem. The remnants of Karel Mollen's last hut (1925) are on the estate Valkenhorst, Valkenswaard.

29 The rufterhood was made of soft, pliable leather, the opening for the falcon's beak wide, so as to enable the bird to throw its casting (see note 71). This type of hood was used during the first days of the training, after which it was replaced by a better, more narrow fitting hood.

30 Bumblefoot: swollen feet, caused both by puncture and by internal ailments.

31 These observations of falconers, based on tradition and the catching of thousands of peregrines, should be kept in mind, though modern ornithologists came to other conclusions (Van de Wall, 1981).

32 Anny van Wingerden & P. C. J. M. Bekkers (1988).

33 Van Oorschot (1974).

34 See Origin of the Club.

35 Van Gerven (1971).

36 Lure: device to keep a flying falcon under control; can be compared with a dog's whistle. It resembles a bird, fastened to a line and activated by swinging (see illustration page 66).

37 Arendonk, important centre of falconry near Valkenswaard, but in Belgium (see Goris 1966).

38 Van Oorschot (1974).

39 See chapter The Falcons, hunting techniques.

40 Dovrefjell: Mountain range in Norway, since early times known for its population of gyrfalcons. Mount Knutshö, where flowers from the ice-age were recently found, has an arctic climate. Near Fokstua falconers' huts were found (Solberg, 1952). Fokstuamyrene is a very large bird sanctuary (Kvaerne, 1968) in the vicinity of Hjerkinn and Mount Knutshö. When closely attending field trials, the author often observed gyrfalcons that were rather tame. However, their waiting-on over trainer and dog was low and poor, contrary to wild peregrines that easily and successfully adapted themselves to waiting on over wildfowler and partridge hunter, when shooting over dogs (Van de Wall, 1980).

41 King Louis Napoleon, contrary to his brother Napoleon Bonaparte, was a man of culture and loved falconry.

42 Both Lascelles (1894) and Swaen (1937) state that the arrest took place at Cuxhafen, Germany. The author, however, assumes the version of Schlegel and Verster van Wulverhorst to be correct. Cuxhafen was beyond the jurisdiction of King Louis. Frans van den Heuvel knew Daems personally, both being in the same English service during the years before 1808. Jan Bots also belonged to the same company of falconers. Moreover, it is clear that in the small community of Valkenswaard the falconers had close contact with one another and met regularly.

43 Research Lady L. R. M. van Everdingen-Meyer, Archives Nationales, Paris.

44 Geographic classification during the French occupation. Today, Valkenswaard is situated in the Province of Brabant, near the Belgian border.

45 According to Salvin & Brodrick (1971), this bag came into the possession of the Duke of Leeds.

46 Major Hawkins Fisher (1901) published a fine photographic portrait of John Pells.

47 The chronology is not clear. According to Van Oorschot (1974), Bots and his pupil Adriaan Mollen already went to France in 1828 into the service of Baron d'Offémont, after which, at the request of Lord Berners, they entered the service of the Falconers' Club in 1833. Maybe Bots returned in 1838 to d'Offémont, but anyhow he started his activities at The Loo in 1839.

48 Saker falcon: *Falco cherrug*. Desert falcon in use by Arabian falconers from time immemorial.

49 Tiercel: Male birds of prey, particularly of falcons, goshawks and sparrowhawks. Their size is approximately two-thirds of that of the females. Deducted from Latin *tertius* meaning one-third.

50 Stone curlew: *Burrhinus oedicnemicus*.

51 Van Oorschot (1974).

52 Today, the Amsterdam Zoo is simply known as "Artis."

53 Budel: hamlet in the vicinity of Valkenswaard.

54 Anny van Wingerden & P. C. J. M. Bekkers (1988).

55 Idem.

VI The Falcons

56 Ratcliffe (1982).

57 Cade (1982).

58 There are many examples of peregrines making their autumn and winter residence in cities, for example Amsterdam.

59 Saar (1975), Cade (1982).

60 Bysterveld (1970).

61 Idem.

62 The saying is that a peregrine "is as round as an apple." Lascelles (1899).

63 Van de Beek (1988).

64 Nora Croin Michielsen (1988).

65 Jack (1970).

66 Dijkstra (1968, 1974, 1975), Morel (1977, 1988). Morel (1979, 1988).

67 Mavrogordato (1966).

68 Lanner falcon, desert falcon, *Falco biarmicus*.

69 Gilbert Blaine. Upton (1980, 1987) pays much attention to this famous falconer.

VII Zoë

I Wolf used the work of his colleague Dubourcq in a way that today is called plagiarism. In their times, however, people were rather liberal in this respect.

II Tuijn published in 1995 about the *Traité de Fauconnerie*. In 2000 followed his contribution in *Joseph Wolf 1820–1899*, an extensive study comprising the Wolf letters. See literature. This exceptionally beautiful illustrated catalogue was edited in connection with the Wolf exhibitions at:

Biohistoricum, Neuburg, Germany
Hessisches Landesmuseum, Germany
Natuurhistorisch Museum Naturalis, Leiden, Netherlands
The Natural History Museum, London, England

VIII Training and Maintenance

70 The condition of the falcon is comparable to that of an athlete. Hunger strongly depresses activity. A hungry bird is not likely to leave the falconer, the lure being more attractive than a flying prey. A hawk with a healthy appetite will and can fly and hunt with great zeal and endurance. Nothing is more attractive to it than a palatable victim in full flight. Fat hawks are lazy and refuse to fly at all, unless to seek comfortable and often inaccessible accommodation in which to rest at leisure and contemplate the world. Falconers speak about a low and a high condition, always aiming at the latter.

71 Casting: pellet consisting of felted feathers or hair, thrown up approximately twelve hours after consuming prey. See note 29.

72 Adriaan Mollen and his son Karel stuffed birds, Newcome was well known for his fine preparations. The museum Felua at Apeldoorn still has in its collection a falcon prepared by Adriaan Mollen, which he presented in 1880 to Mrs. Bloemink, former proprietress of the New Crown, see page 72. One of the descendants of Verster van Wulverhorst still has a preparation of a hooded falcon in his possession. At the Aardhuis, King William's former shooting lodge near the Echoput, a falcon on a heron is exhibited (see illustration page 79).

73 Screenperch: the screen was devised to enable the falcon to climb back, when frightened, disturbed or trying to flee. To an unhooded falcon the screenperch is safe when it is well manned (see illustration page 62).

74 Lascelles (1899).

75 Hood: designed to obstruct the bird's vision completely so as to keep it quiet under all

circumstances. Braces enable the falconer to reduce the circumference fitting around the neck (hooding) or enlarge it to unhood. "No man can claim to be a master of hawks until he is master of the art of hooding; he who has perfected himself in this art has gained the whole secret of his falcon." (Blaine, 1936). When properly handled, falcons have not the slightest objection to being hooded.

76 Cadge: rectangular "screenperch" which offers a perch to a number of hawks and is carried by means of straps across the shoulders of the falconer (see page 42).

77 Hack: period wherein young hawks are flying in a semi-wild state to build up strength and flight techniques, so as to gain as far as possible the qualities of the wild falcon. On indication of Bots and Mollen elaborately described in *Traité de Fauconnerie*.

78 Flying at hack in those times and later was not practised in Valkenswaard.

79 Pointer meaning pointing dog; for examble setter, pointer of some continental races.

80 Creance: line used in the first part of the training, when it was not yet safe to allow the falcon complete freedom.

81 Shortly before his death, Karel Mollen, son of Adriaan, told the author that he too used cockerels during the training of passage falcons, destined for the rook-hawking parties of the Old Hawking Club in England.

IX À la Vol et à la Volte

82 À la Vol. Strictly, À le Vol = Au Vol. Though linguistically wrong, the term was indeed À la Vol and known as such in French literature. Information revealed that sometimes such alterations are allowed in French. Salvin & Brodrick (1971), however, spoke about Au Vol.

83 Roger Tory Peterson, illustrator and co-author of the *Field Guide to Birds of Britain and Europe*. Quoted by Cade (1982).

84 According to Oltmans (1923), the last wolves on the Veluwe were seen in approximately 1760.

85 Van Es (1908) quoted from the diary of Count Dumonceau, in 1852, adjutant to King William III. He attended the flights not as a member of the Club, but in his function as adjutant.

86 In 1846 Newcome took along a trained cormorant for Salvin, a well-known falconer and ornithologist (Upton, 1980).

87 These young falcons were caught late in the season, probably December of the foregoing year and so had not completed their training when the Haut Vol season started.

88 Chien de Terre Neuve, New Foundlander. Probably the Prince meant Labrador retriever, a British race, today gaining the status of a clearly defined race.

89 The falconers were sometimes dressed in uniform, designed at the time of the adept of falconry, the French King Louis XIII. Generally, however, they are pictured in uniform with cap or in dress with top hat. A letter of February 26, 1850, from Mollen, addressed to Anemaet, reads: "We will soon send you the measurements which will be taken at Eindhoven, because there is nobody here who can do it. So we shall make sure that they will reach you within two or three days."

90 Weighing scales were not yet used in falconry. Today they are of help in determining the condition of the birds.

91 Evers (1913) tells us that poor people attended the flights to gather a meal of fresh fish.

92 Pichot (1865).

93 Dumonceau, see note 85. It was, however, very unlikely that, two falcons being in action, a second couple was slipped to assist.

94 In the collection of the State Museum of Natural History at Leiden, there are three gyrfalcons which in the years 1842 and 1843 belonged to Prince Alexander and were active at The Loo. Probably Zoë is one of them, but could not be conclusively identified as such.

X The Reporters

95 H. Schlegel: lit. Hubrecht (1884), Schlegel J. (1884), Snelleman (1884), Van Es (1908), Thierfelder (1963), Kosten (1967).

96 This letter was certainly meant for Prince Alexander, President of the Club, and not for his father King William II, who was not in the least interested in the sport.

97 A. Verster van Wulverhorst: lit. H. Schlegel (1854), Brouwer (1950), Van Oorschot (1974).

98 J. Wolf: lit. Palmer (1895).

99 His handwriting betrays his former activities as a designer of wine labels. The correspondence mentioned is in the library of the University of Leiden.

100 Reid Henry (1976).

XI Downfall and End of the Club

101 Velp, village and summer resort alongside the Ijssel River, near Arnhem.

102 Boer (1939). Already at this time screw-propelled steamers were in service between Holland and England.

103 It is very doubtful whether the falconers could make use of the ice cellar of the palace.

104 Van Oorschot (1974).

105 Personal communication Roger Upton.

106 Haasse & Jackman (1984), letter of June 23rd, 1852. See also note 26.

107 Van Es (1908).

108 Mollerus: The following proceedings were reconstructed from correspondence, present in the family archives of G. W. Baron Mollerus. Henry Marie Baron Mollerus was born in Amsterdam on September 24, 1812. His father being ambassador, his education chiefly took place in foreign countries. In 1835, he was appointed attaché in Vienna and so we find his stamp on Mollen's passport when en route to Prince Trautmannsdorf. In 1843, he became chamberlain to the King and settled in The Hague. At his own request, he was relieved of his functions in 1855. He then left the country to settle in Potsdam, where he married Hélène von Bülow in 1862. She died in 1866 and he remarried Anna

von Wiechert in 1869. The pair settled in Gries near Bolzano. Mollerus died in 1899, his widow in 1941.

109 In 1850, the membership roll counted sixty-one members.

110 Van Oorschot (1974), quoted literally.

111 Van Oorschot (1974).

112 See note 53.

113 This appears from a letter from Mr. Weslye Egeberg of Christiania (Oslo today), August 2, 1841, and addressed to Baron Verstolk van Soelen, Secretary of Foreign Affairs at The Hague. The day before Bots had arrived by steamer and, as requested on July 8, he had furnished him the necessary means to travel to Hjerkinn to catch gyrfalcons. In this letter, Bots was named as falconer to Prince Alexander. As far as we know, this was the last time a Dutch falconer went to Dovrefjell to catch gyrfalcons.

114 Van Es (1908) mentions that in 1853, owing to repeated cuts in expenditure, only the falconers A. Mollen, P. Bekkers and P. Mollen were still in service. But there is room for doubt. On July 1, 1854, Mollerus, functioning as the Club's administrator, requested the Secretary of the Interior to issue new licences to both Adriaan Mollen, falconer to the King, and to his subordinates Paulus Mollen, Petrus Bekkers, Johannes van den Boom and Lambertus Peels to catch falcons on their own property or on property of others who were agreeable, to train them at herons by means of pigeons.

115 Lascelles (1899).

Concluding Words

116 The developments as described in the concluding words are strictly confined to conditions in western Europe. The author cannot claim sufficient insight into developments outside this area.

117 The concluding words could also refer to the austringers' art of hawking, training goshawk and sparrowhawk. These birds have gained more appraisal of late. The number of austringers today is surpassing by far that of falconers.

Appendices

Appendix 1

Membership roll of the Royal Loo Hawking Club
President and Patron HRH King William III

Patroness
HM the Queen of Holland

Honorary Members
HRH the Prince of Wales
HRH Prince Albert
HRH Prince George of Cambridge.

Members

1839 Duke of Leeds
Baron Tindal
Baron van Capellen
Baron V. van Tuyll van Serooskerken+
Baron d'Offémont
Hon. C. Stuart Wortley
E. C. Newcome Esq. +
Sir Joseph Copley

1840 HRH Prince Henry
HRH Prince Frederick
Baron van Nijvenheim
W. A. Baron Schimmelpenninck van der Oye
Hon. H. Steengracht van Oosterland
Baron van Zuylen van Nievelt van de Schaffelaar
General Baron van Nahuys Burgst
Mr. A. van der Hoop
H. Baron Schimmelpenninck van der Oye
Mr. van Loon
Mr. Huydecoper van Zeist
Baron van Brienen van de Groote Lindt
Sir Edward Cromwell Disbrowe
Sir Alex. Mallet BT+
Hon. W. S. Jerningham
Mr. Fabricius van Leyenburg en Heukelom
Mr. W. Newcome Esq.
Baron Sloet van Toutenburg
Baron Sloet van Oldruitenborgh Secr.
Lord Willoughby d'Eresby
Evelyn Dennison Esq.
Lord Cranstoun
Prince Esterhazy
W. P. Barnaart van Bergen
Baron van Rhenen
Mr. Hodson
Mr. Brugmans
Count von Rantzow
Baron Sirtema van Grovenstins, Treas.
Baron de Constant Rebeque
Count von Willich und Lottum
W. Newcome
Baron von Trautmannsdorf
Sir Edward Beaumont
Sir Hume Huge Campbell

1841 Baron von Otterstedt
Sir Horace Hammond

Portraits in watercolour by J. Sonderland, approx. 32 x 33 cm in Royal House Archive.

1842 Lord Claude Hamilton
Mr. Edward Humphrey Greene
Lord Suffield
Hon. W. Twisselton Fiennes
J. Wellesley Esq.
J. T. Hales Tooke
Edward Humphrys Greene
J. Balfour
E. H. Dennison Esq.
A. Foster Esq.
R. Knightly
Earl of Kinnoul
Lord Loftus
W. H. Gregory Esq.

1843 Baron van Westreenen van Driebergen+
Baron van Verschuer+
H. C. Dubois+
Baron von Gablentz+
Sir John Hammer
Mr. Millbank+

1844 Mr. W. S. Stirling Crawfurd
Baron Amédée van den Bogaerde
Baron Mollerus
Lord Alvanly
Baron van Hardenbroek
Lord Earl of Chesterfield
Mr. D. J. C. van Lennep
Mr. W. Ellis
Count Westerholt
Mr. J. Borski
Mr. John Melvil

1845 Count Noailles
Baron van den Bogaerde (see 1844)
Mollerus (see 1844)
Sir Horace Seymour
Count Alfred von Hatzfeld
Baron van Tuyll van Serooskerken van Vleuten
Mr. D. J. C. van Lennep (see 1844)
Mr. Crommelin
Baron van Brakel van Doorwerth

1846 Major-General Hare Clarges
Baron von Knobelsdorf van Hamerstein
Mr. Thornhill
Count Breteuil

1847 Major Mountjoy Martin
Lord Villiers
Lord Earl of Strathmore
HRH the Duke of Nassau
Mr. Gudin+
Mr. Fred Millbank (see 1843)
Mr. Meynard

1848 Count Esterhazy
Baron C. J. van Tuyll van Serooskerken
Count Karl zu Elz
Frederik Baron Breidbach-Bürresheim

	Mr. James Brown	
	Hon. Louis de Bogaerde (see 1845)	
	Mr. Robert Clifton	
	Mr. J. F. Rowlands	
	Baron de Pfeill	
1849	Lord Earl Cadogan	
	Mr. J. P. A. van Wickevoort Crommelin	
	E. L. Baron van Tuyll van Serooskerken van Vleuten	
	Mr. Petre	
	Right Hon. Sir Watkinn W. Wynn	
	H. Grace the Duke of Cleveland	
	H. Grace the Duke of Rutland	
	Lord Earl of Eylinton and Winton	
	Mr. H. A. van Karnebeek	
	General Boreel	
	Count Alfred de Noailles	
1850	Baron de Lareinty	
	Count Bentinck	
	Total number of members: 124.	

It is conspicuous that items concerning the membership list regarding the period 1850–1855 were not found in the archives.

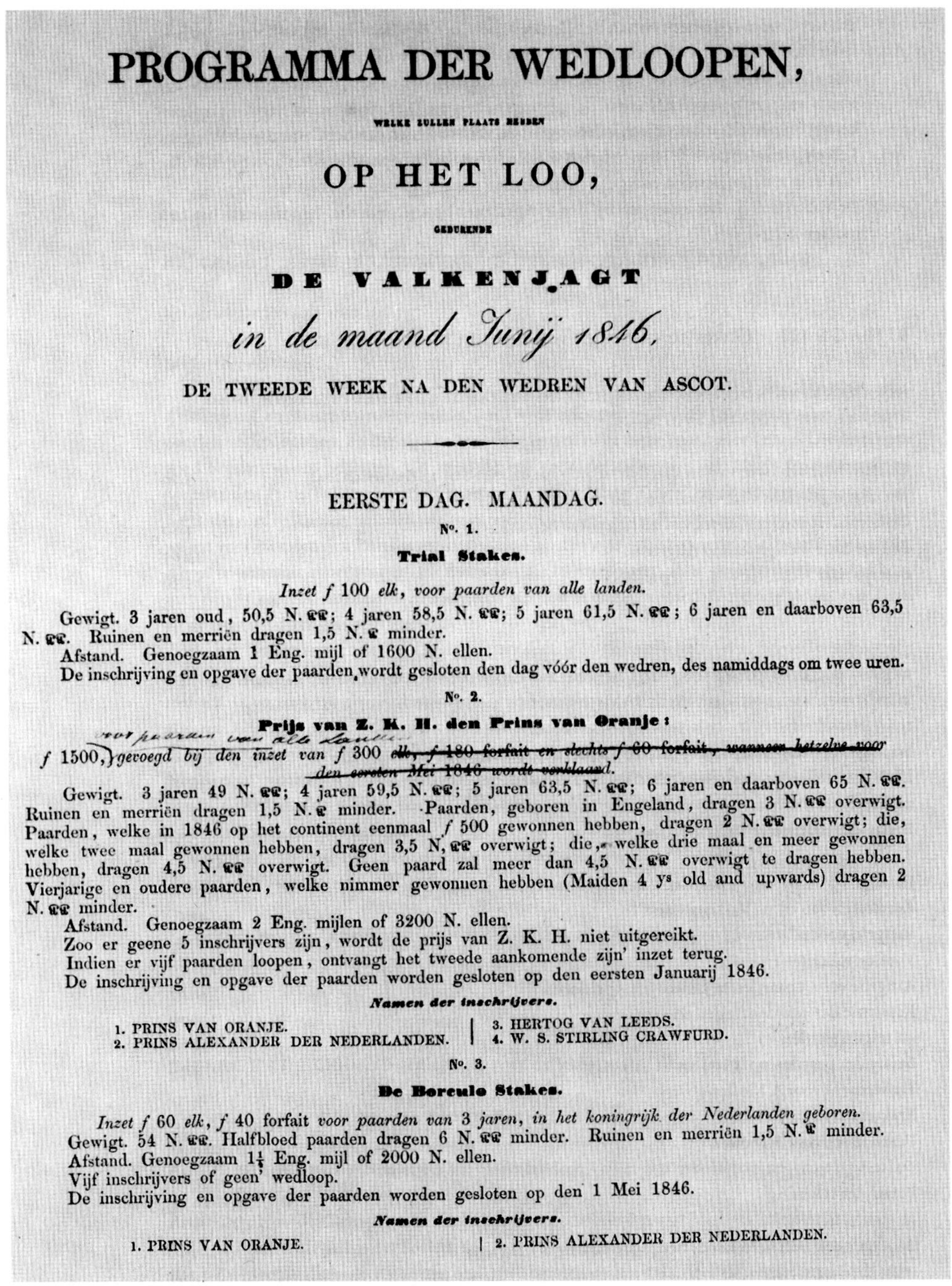

PROGRAMMA DER WEDLOOPEN,

WELKE ZULLEN PLAATS HEBBEN

OP HET LOO,

GEDURENDE

DE VALKENJAGT

in de maand Junij 1846,

DE TWEEDE WEEK NA DEN WEDREN VAN ASCOT.

EERSTE DAG. MAANDAG.

N°. 1.

Trial Stakes.

Inzet f 100 *elk, voor paarden van alle landen.*

Gewigt. 3 jaren oud, 50,5 N. ℔℔; 4 jaren 58,5 N. ℔℔; 5 jaren 61,5 N. ℔℔; 6 jaren en daarboven 63,5 N. ℔℔. Ruinen en merriën dragen 1,5 N. ℔ minder.

Afstand. Genoegzaam 1 Eng. mijl of 1600 N. ellen.

De inschrijving en opgave der paarden wordt gesloten den dag vóór den wedren, des namiddags om twee uren.

N°. 2.

Prijs van Z. K. H. den Prins van Oranje:

f 1500, *voor paarden van alle landen* gevoegd bij den inzet van *f* 300 ~~elk, *f* 180 forfait en slechts *f* 60 forfait, wanneer hetzelve voor den eersten Mei 1846 wordt verklaard~~.

Gewigt. 3 jaren 49 N. ℔℔; 4 jaren 59,5 N. ℔℔; 5 jaren 63,5 N. ℔℔; 6 jaren en daarboven 65 N. ℔℔. Ruinen en merriën dragen 1,5 N. ℔ minder. Paarden, geboren in Engeland, dragen 3 N. ℔℔ overwigt. Paarden, welke in 1846 op het continent eenmaal *f* 500 gewonnen hebben, dragen 2 N. ℔℔ overwigt; die, welke twee maal gewonnen hebben, dragen 3,5 N. ℔℔ overwigt; die, welke drie maal en meer gewonnen hebben, dragen 4,5 N. ℔℔ overwigt. Geen paard zal meer dan 4,5 N. ℔℔ overwigt te dragen hebben. Vierjarige en oudere paarden, welke nimmer gewonnen hebben (Maiden 4 ys old and upwards) dragen 2 N. ℔℔ minder.

Afstand. Genoegzaam 2 Eng. mijlen of 3200 N. ellen.

Zoo er geene 5 inschrijvers zijn, wordt de prijs van Z. K. H. niet uitgereikt.

Indien er vijf paarden loopen, ontvangt het tweede aankomende zijn' inzet terug.

De inschrijving en opgave der paarden worden gesloten op den eersten Januarij 1846.

Namen der inschrijvers.

1. PRINS VAN ORANJE.
2. PRINS ALEXANDER DER NEDERLANDEN.
3. HERTOG VAN LEEDS.
4. W. S. STIRLING CRAWFURD.

N°. 3.

De Borculo Stakes.

Inzet f 60 *elk, f* 40 forfait *voor paarden van* 3 *jaren, in het koningrijk der Nederlanden geboren.*

Gewigt. 54 N. ℔℔. Halfbloed paarden dragen 6 N. ℔℔ minder. Ruinen en merriën 1,5 N. ℔ minder.

Afstand. Genoegzaam $1\frac{1}{4}$ Eng. mijl of 2000 N. ellen.

Vijf inschrijvers of geen' wedloop.

De inschrijving en opgave der paarden worden gesloten op den 1 Mei 1846.

Namen der inschrijvers.

1. PRINS VAN ORANJE.
2. PRINS ALEXANDER DER NEDERLANDEN.

Appendix 2:

Programme of a horse race, 1846.

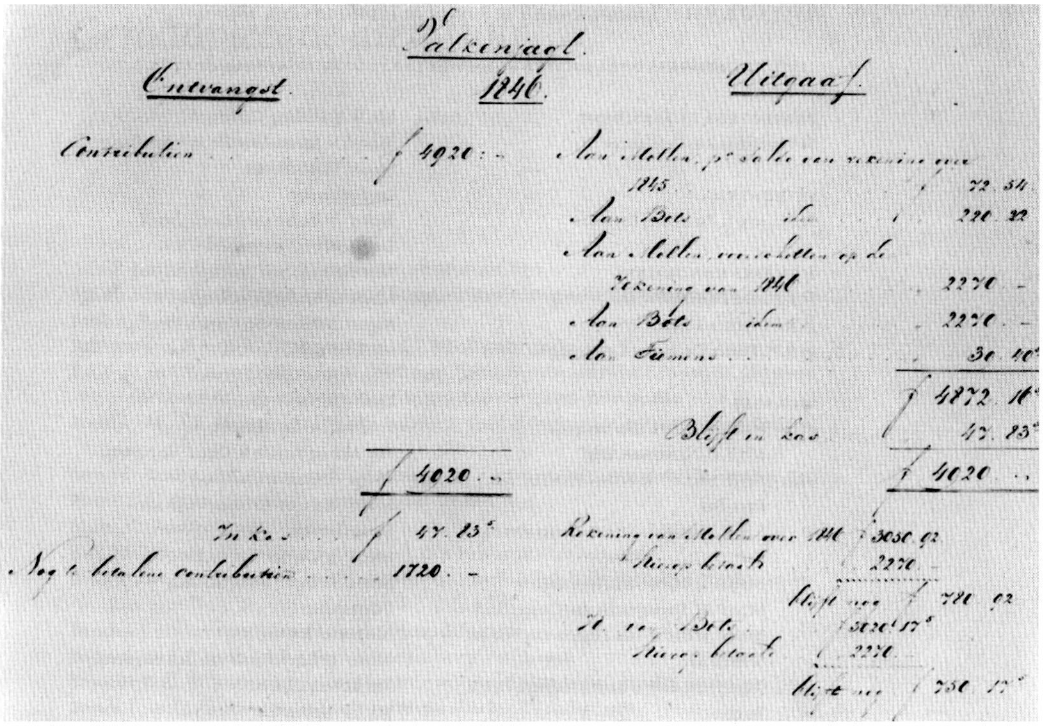

Valkenswaard.

Ontvangst.	1846.	Uitgaaf.	
Contributien	f 4020:-	Aan Mollen, pr saldo van rekening over 1845	f 72.54
		Aan Bots idem	220.22
		Aan Mollen voorschotten op de rekening van 1846	2270.-
		Aan Bots idem	2270.-
		Aan Firmans	30.40
			f 4872.16
		Blijft in Kas	47.83
	f 4020.-		f 4020.-
In Kas	f 47.83	Rekening van Mollen over 1846	f 3050.92
Nog te betalene contributien	1720.-	Hierop betaald	2270.-
		Blijft nog	f 780.92
		Id. van Bots	f 3020.17
		Hierop betaald	2270.-
		Blijft nog	f 750.17

Appendix 3:

Programme of a horse race, 1846.

Literature

Aa, A. J. van der, *Ons Vaderland en zijne Bewoners*. Amsterdam, 1857.

Agassiz Fuertes, L., "Falconry the Sport of Kings," in *National Geographic Magazine* XXXVIII.

Baldick, R., *The Duel*. London, 1970.

Bannermann, D. A., *Birds of the British Isles*, Vol. V. Edinburgh, 1955.

Bas, F. de en C. W. A. van Haersolte van den Doorn,: "Levensbericht van N. J. A. P. H. van Es," Overdruk uit de *Levensberichten van de Maatschappij der Nederlandse Letterkunde*. Leiden, 1921.

Beaszly, J. M., A. K. Manners, A. C. White-Robinson, *Training Setters and Pointers for Fieldtrials*. London, 1973.

Beek, E. van de, "Aerodynamics in brief of Bird's Flight." *Yearbook 50th anniversary of the Netherlands Valkeniersverbond Adriaan Mollen*. Engl. Summary

Bert, Edmunt, *Bert's Treatise of Hawks and Hawking*, 1619. Facsimile uitgegeven door J. E. Hatting, 1891.

Blaine, D. P., *An Encyclopedia of British Rural Sports*. London, 1856.

Blaine, G., *Falconry*. London, 1936.

Boer, M. G. de, 100 Jaar Nederlandsche Scheepvaart. Den Helder/Amsterdam, 1939.

Bornewasser, J. A. "Koning Willem II" in *Nassau en Oranje in de Nederlandse Geschiedenis*. Alphen aan den Rijn, 1977.

Bosscha, J. *Het leven van Willem den Tweede*. Amsterdam, 1852.

Boyer, A. en P. Planiol, *Traité de Fauconnerie et Autourserie*. Paris, 1948.

Brouwer, G. A., "Historische gegevens over onze vroegere ornithologen," in *Ardea*, January, 1950.

Brown, L. en D. Amadon, *Eagles, Hawks and Falcons of the World*. London, 1968.

Bysterveld, O. P. van, "De gezichtsscherpte van roofvogels," in *Jaarboek van het Nederlands Valkeniersverbond Adriaan Mollen*, 1970.

Cade, T., *The Falcons of the World*. London, 1982.

Chamerlat, G. A. de, *Falconry and Art*, Sotheby's Publications, 1987.

In France A. C. R. Edition Vilo, *La Fauconnerie et l'Art*.

Croin Michielsen, Nora, "How fast do our birds of prey fly and do Peregrine Falcon and Goshawk drop from the skies like a stone?" *Yearbook 50th anniversary of the Netherlands Valkeniersverbond Adriaan Mollen*. Engl. Summary

Daendels, H. A., Valkerij in het Veld (Falconry in the field). Ed. *Dutch Museum of Game and Game-Management*. Doorwerth, Netherlands, 1988.

Dale, J. H. van, *Groot Woordenboek der Nederlandse Taal*. 's Gravenhage, 1969.

Dam, J. H., "De Nederlandse valkerij-literatuur," in *Jaarboek van het Nederlands Valkeniersverbond Adriaan Mollen*. 1968.

Delmé Radcliffe, E., *Notes on the Falconideae used in India in Falconry*, 1875. Facsimile Prampton on Severn, 1971.

Dementiev, G. P., *Der Gerfalke*. Wittenberg, 1960.

Dijkstra, H., *International Ornithological Bulletin The Ring*. Vol. 2, no. 16, August, 1958.

Idem, "Aanwachters," in *Jaarboek van het Nederlands Valkeniersverbond Adriaan Mollen*. 1968.

Idem, "Aanwachten in Spanje," in *Jaarboek van het Nederlands Valkeniersverbond Adriaan Mollen*. 1974.

Idem, "Problemen en ervaringen in de aanwachterij," in *Jaarboek van het Nederlands Valkeniersverbond Adriaan Mollen*. 1975.

Idem, "Revalidatie van een trekkende slechtvalk," in *Jaarboek van het Nederlands Valkeniersverbond Adriaan Mollen*, 1980.

Doorn, Jacqueline, *Willem III, Emma en Sophie*. Zaltbommel, 1977.

Es, N. J. A. P. H. van, *De Hippische Sport en het Korps Rijdende Artillerie. Deel 1: De Valkerij in Europa sinds de vroegste tijden*. Arnhem, 1908.

Everdingen, L. van, "De Vorsten van Oranje en de Valkerij," in *Jaarboek van het Nederlands Valkeniersverbond Adriaan Mollen*. 1981.

Evers, G. A., "De jacht op de Soerensche Daghuurders," in *Buiten*, jrg. 7. 1913.

Fisher, H. C., *Reminiscences of a falconer*. London, 1901.

Fox, N. C., "Condition in Hawks," in *The Falconer, The Journal of the British Falconers' Club*, 1980.

Freeman, G. A., *Practical Falconry (How I became a Falconer)*. London, 1869.

Fyfe, R., "Observations on Tundra Peregrine and Gyrfalcon from Southampton Island, NWT," in *The Journal of the North American Falconers Association*, Vol. 1, no. 1. 1962.

Gerven, J. van, "Uit Valkenswaards Familiebezit," in *Jaarboek van het Nederlands Valkeniersverbond Adriaan Mollen*. 1970.

Idem, "Uit Valkenswaards Familiebezit II," in *Jaarboek van het Nederlands Valkeniersverbond Adriaan Mollen. 1*971.

Haasse, H., en S. W. Jackman, *Een vreemdelinge in Den Haag, uit de brieven van Koningin Sophie der Nederlanden aan Lady Malet*. Amsterdam, 1984.

Hermans, A. G. J., *Jagerswoordenboek*. Schiedam, 1947.

Herren, H., "Released Raptors," in *The Falconer, The Journal of the British Falconers' Club*, 1970.

Hubrecht, A. A. W., "Hermann Schlegel," in *De Gids* no. 3. 1884.

Illingworth, F., *Falcons and Falconry*. London, 195?.

Jack, T. A. M., "Hawk Sense," part II, in *The Falconer, The Journal of the British Falconers' Club*. 1970.

Idem, "Hawk Sense, Visibility," in *The Falconer, The Journal of the British Falconers' Club*. 1973.

Kenward, R. E., "Birds of Prey: the facts of life and death," in *The Falconer, The Journal of the British Falconers' Club*. 1974.

Kleinschmidt, O., *Berajah, Zoographia Infinita*. Halle a. d. Saale, 1923–1937.

Kosten, A. P. W. M., Scriptie over Hermann Schlegel en het Rijksmuseum van Natuurlijke Historie. Leiden, 1976 (aanwezig: Rijksmuseum van Natuurlijke Historie).

Kvaerne, M., *Along the King's Highway*. Oslo, 1966.

Lascelles, G., *Falconry in Coursing and Falconry*. London, 1899.

Lennep, J. van, en W. J. Hofdijk, *Merkwaardige Kastelen in Nederland*. Amsterdam, 1854.

Lindner, K., *Bibliographie der deutschen und der niederländischen Jagdliteratur von 1480 bis 1850*. Berlijn/New York, 1976.

Magelhaes, C., *Nederlandse Fotographie de eerste honderd jaar*. Bruna & Zn. Utrecht-Antwerpen, 1969.

Mathis, M., "La Chasse au Faucon en Tunisie," in *Bulletin de la Société des Sciences Naturelles de Tunisie*, Vol. II, no. 3–4. 1949.

Mattox, W. G., "Baker Library and The Sport of Kings," in *Dartmouth College Library Bulletin*, Vol. XII, no. 1. November 1971.

Idem, "Banding Gyrfalcons (*Falco Rusticolus*) in Greenland, 1967," in *Bird-Banding*, Vol. 41, no. 1. January 1970.

Mavrogordato, J. G., *A Hawk for the Bush*. London, 1960.

Idem, *A Falcon in the Field*. London, 1966.

Mercier, L., *La Chasse et les Sports chez les Arabes*. Paris, 1927.

Michaëlis, H. von, *Birds of the Gauntlet*. London, 1952.

Michell, E. B., *The Art and Practice of Hawking*. London, 1900.

Morel, P., "Het aanwachten in België," in *Jaarboek van het Nederlands Valkeniersverbond Adriaan Mollen. 1979*.

Mowat, F., *Ordeal by Ice; The Search for the North West Passage*. Toronto, 1977.

Nie, G. A. van, "Enkele grepen uit de geschiedenis van het Nederlands Valkeniersverbond Adriaan Mollen," in *Jaarboek van het Nederlands Valkeniersverbond Adriaan Mollen.* 1970, 1971, 1973, 1976, 1978.

Idem, "Een merkwaardig plaatje," in *Jaarboek van het Nederlands Valkeniersverbond Adriaan Mollen. 1977*.

Nie, G. J. van, "Congres over beheerstechnieken bij roofvogels, Oxford," in *Jaarboek van het Nederlands Valkeniersverbond Adriaan Mollen. 1977*.

Niesters, H., "Voor het eerst slaagden valkeniers er in de Amerikaanse witkopzeearend (*Haliaetus leukocephalus*) te fokken," in *Jaarboek van het Nederlands Valkeniersverbond Adriaan Mollen. 1979.*

Oltmans, A. B., "De strijd tegen de wolven op de Veluwe," in *Bijdragen en Mededelingen*, DXVI. Arnhem, 1923.

Oorschot, J. M. P. van, *Vorstelijke Vliegers en Valkenswaardse Valkeniers*. Dissertatie, Tilburg, 1974.

Idem, "De valk tussen leeuwerik en Gallische Haan," in *Jaarboek van het Nederlands Valkeniersverbond Adriaan Mollen. 1974.*

Idem, "De hoge vlucht van de valk in het Duitse taalgebied," in *Jaarboek van het Nederlands Valkeniersverbond Adriaan Mollen. 1975.*

Opdam, P., "De technocratie van een valkenier of Het Recht om Wild te zijn," in *Jaarboek van het Nederlands Valkeniersverbond Adriaan Mollen. 1974.*

Idem, *De Havik*. Utrecht/Antwerpen, 1978.

Orton, D. A., "The speed of a peregrine's drive," in *The Field*. 25 September 1975.

Idem, "Falcon v. Raven v. Vixen at nest," in *The Field*. 8 July 1976.

Idem, "Peregrines at the point of kill," in *The Field*. 16 April 1980.

Palmer, A. H., *The life of Joseph Wolf, Animal Painter*. London, 1895.

Pichot, P. M. H., *La Fauconnerie en Angleterre et en France à notre époque*. Paris, 1865.

Ratcliffe, D., *The Peregrine Falcon*. Calton, 1980.

Reid-Henry, D. M. "Kite Hawking by Joseph Wolf," in *The Falcon, The Journal of the British Falconers' Club*. 1967.

Roorda, M., "Van Heeckeren verijdelde 's Konings huwelijksplan," *Maandblad Vorsten*. August, 1989.

Rose, R. N., *The Field,* 1853–1953. London, 1953.

Saar, Chr., "Die Zucht von Wanderfalken. Ein Beitrag zum Überleben einer vom Aussterben bedrohten Art," in *Jahresbericht des Zool*. Gartens, Berlin, 1975.

Idem, G. Trommer en W. Hammer, *Der Wanderfalke, Bericht über ein Artenschutzprogramm - Methoden, Ziele und Erfolge*. Löningen, 1982.

Salvin, F. H. en W. Brodrick, *Falconry in the British Isles*. London, 1855. Facsimile Maidenhead, 1971.

Schlegel, H. en A. H. Verster van Wulverhorst, *Traité de Fauconnerie*, Leiden/Düsseldorf, 1853.

Idem, *Traité de Fauconnerie*. Bewerking van H. Brüll. Lausanne, 1978.

Idem, *Traité de Fauconnerie*, facsimile New York, 1979 (inleiding van F. L. S. Gavin Bridson).

Schlegel, H., "De wolf onder de schapen," in *Jaarboek van het Koninklijk Zoölogisch Gezelschap Natura Artis Magistra*. 1854.

Idem, *De Vogels van Nederland*. Amsterdam, 1878.

Schlegel, J., "Levensschets van Hermann Schlegel," in *Jaarboek der Koninklijke Akademie van Wetenschappen*. 1884.

Schulz-Hagen, K. & Geus, A., *Joseph Wolf (1920–1899)*, Basilisken Presse, Marburg a. d. Lahn, Germany, 2001.
Slijper, H. J., "Uniek Nederlands traktaat over africhting en verzorging van jachtvogels (16e eeuw)," in *Jaarboek van het Nederlands Valkeniersverbond Adriaan Mollen. 1*981.
Slijper, H. J., "The sketches of the painter Dubourcq made for the album Croquis de la Chasse," *Yearbook 50th anniversary of the Netherlands Valkeniersverbond Adriaan Mollen*. Engl. Summary.
Snelleman, J. F., H. Schlegel. *Mannen van betekenis in onze dagen*. Haarlem, 1884.
Solberg, A., "Dovrefjell," in *Den Norske Turistforenings Årbok*. 1952.
Staal, J. D. M., "Falco Columbarius of avonturen met een smelleken," in *Jaarboek van het Nederlands Valkeniersverbond Adriaan Mollen. 1*976.
Stevens, R., *Observations on Modern Falconry*. Shrewsbury, 1956.
Idem, *The Taming of Genghis*. London, 1956.
Stockum, W. P. van, *La Fauconnerie (chasse au vol)*. Den Haag, 1840.
Stoet, F. A., *Nederlandsche Spreekwoorden en Gezegden*. Zutphen, 1928.
Swaen, A. E. H., *De Valk in de Iconographie*. Maastricht, 1926.
Idem, *Beknopte Woordenlijst der Valkenierstaal*. Deventer, z. j.
Idem, *De Cura Accipitrum*. Groningen, 1937.
Idem, *De Valkerij in de Nederlanden*. Zutphen, 1937.
Tamse, C. A., "Koning Willem III en Sophie," in *Nassau en Oranje in de Nederlandse Geschiedenis*. Alphen aan den Rijn, 1977.
Thierfelder, F., "H. Schlegel," in *Abhandlungen u. Berichte des Naturkundlichen Museum 'Mauritianum'Altenburg*. Bnd. III. 1963.
Tillisch, C. J., *Falkejagten og dens Historie*. Kopenhagen, 1949.
Turner, A. and Hasler, *A Gamehawk*. Gallery Press, Lavenham, 1996.
Tuyn, P., *On the Traité de Fauconnerie*. Reprint from QUERENDO, 25, 4. 1995. Ed. E. J.
Tuijn, P. "Zoë, a gyrfalcon" in *Schulze-Hagen & Geus Armin*, 2001. Brill, 2300 PA Leiden, the Netherlands.
Tuyn, P., *Catalogue of the Falconry Exhibition, Dutch Museum of Game and Game-Management*, Doorwer, 1988.
Upton, R., *A Bird in the Hand*. London, 1980.
Upton, Roger, *O for a Falconer's Voice*. Marlborough, 1987.
Verster van Wulverhorst, A. H., "Over de jagt met den vogel in Nederland," in *Nederlandsch Tijdschrift voor Liefhebbers der Jagt en Visscherij*. 3e jaargang, 1855.
Valkenjagt, *Nederlandsch Museum*, 13e deel. Amsterdam, 1848.
Vogt, Aug. F. W., "Valkenvangst," in *Buiten*, jrg. 33, 1907.
Wall, J. W. M. van de, *Voordracht voor het Nederlands Valkeniersverbond Adriaan Mollen*, gehouden te Amsterdam d. d. 4 October 1947 ter gelegenheid van de hervatting

van de activiteiten na de oorlog. (Aanwezig: archief van het *Nederlands Valkeniersverbond Adriaan Mollen.*)

Idem, In Memoriam Professor Swaen, 1947 (Aanwezig: archief van het *Nederlands Valkeniersverbond Adriaan Mollen*).

Idem, "Kanttekeningen bij de ontwikkeling van de jacht en haar verhouding tot de valkerij," in Jaarboek van het *Nederlands Valkeniersverbond Adriaan Mollen. 1967.*

Idem, "Ontmoetingen met geervalken in de literatuur en in het veld," in *Jaarboek van het Nederlands Valkeniersverbond Adriaan Mollen. 1980.*

Wall, J. W. M. van de, en G. J. van Nie, "Moderne ontwikkelingen in de valkerij," in *Jaarboek van het Nederlands Valkeniersverbond Adriaan Mollen. 1981.*

Van de Wall, J. W. M., "Some observations of the hunting flight of the Peregrine falcon, particularly as regards stooping," *Yearbook 50th anniversary of the Netherlands Valkeniersverbond Adriaan Mollen*. Engl. Summary.

Wall, J. W. M. van de, "De Haut Vol en zijn antipode de Aanwachterij," *Jaarboek Nederlands Valkeniersverbond Adriaan Mollen. 2001.*

Walsh, J. H., *Stonehenge's British Rural Sports*. London, 1881.

Wood, Casey A., en M. Fyfe, *The Art of Falconry being De Arte Venandi cum Avibus of Frederick II von Hohenstauffen*. Stanford, 1943.

Woodford, M. H., "Those were the Days: Falconry in the United Kingdom from 1772 to 1926," in *The Falconer, The Journal of the British Falconers' Club,* 1968.

Zeggelen, W. J. van, *De dichtwerken van W. J. van Zeggelen; De Valkenvangst*. Rotterdam, 1874.

Zijlstra, J., en D. Schakel, "Onderzoek naar waarnemingen van de slechtvalk in Nederland," in *Jaarboek van het Nederlands Valkeniersverbond Adriaan Mollen. 1968.*

Index